HOW TO USE TRUSTS TO AVOID PROBATE AND TAXES

A Guide to Living, Marital, Support, Charitable, and Insurance Trusts

OTHER RANDOM HOUSE LAW MANUALS

HOW TO USE TRUSTS *to* AVOID PROBATE *and* TAXES

A Guide to Living, Marital, Support, Charitable, and Insurance Trusts

THERESA MEEHAN RUDY, KAY OSTBERG and JEAN DIMEO

in Association with HALT

RANDOM HOUSE NEW YORK

This work was originally published in different form as *Trusts:
A Guide to Trust Options for Avoiding Probate and Taxes* by HALT
in 1991.

HALT—An Organization of Americans for Legal Reform, is a national, nonprofit, nonpartisan public interest group with more
than 150,000 members. Based in Washington, D.C., its goals are to
enable people to handle their legal affairs simply, affordably, and
equitably. HALT's education and advocacy programs strive to
improve the quality, reduce the costs and increase the accessibil-
ity of the civil justice system. Its activities are funded by members'
contributions.

Library of Congress Cataloging-in-Publication Data

Rudy, Theresa M.
    How to use trusts to avoid probate and taxes: a guide to
living, marital, support, charitable, and insurance trusts /
Theresa Meehan Rudy, Kay Ostberg, and Jean Dimeo in association with HALT.
        p. cm.—(A Random House practical law manual)
    ISBN 0-679-74127-5
    1. Trusts and trustees—United States—Popular Works.
I. Ostberg, Kay. II. Dimeo, Jean. III. HALT, Inc. IV. Title.
V. Series.
KF730.Z9R83   1992
346.7305'9—dc20
[347.30659]   91-46443   CIP

Book design by Charlotte Staub

Manufactured in the United States of America
1 2 3 4 5 6 7 8 9
First Random House Edition

Contents

Introduction

Chances are you picked up this book because you heard that setting up a trust can help you avoid the cost and delays of probate and prevent you from having much of your property gobbled up by fees and taxes after you die.

What you may not know is that trusts can do a lot more. They can protect your family's inheritance from unforeseen disasters like lawsuits, divorces or fiscally irresponsible heirs. They can ensure that your estate plan stays private, that your personal and financial needs are taken care of if you become incapacitated because of illness or injury, and that your spouse is provided for after you die. These and many more goals can be accomplished through the use of a trust.

In recent years, more and more Americans have set up trusts to take advantage of the flexibility and security trusts offer. The American Bankers Association reports that by 1988 more than 1.5 million Americans had set up personal trust accounts with banking institutions. Although no reliable data are available on how many people set up trusts outside of banks, we know that the demand for information about trusts is at an all-time high.

A WORD ABOUT TERMS

Trust documents are filled with legalese. Words like *corpus, grantor, inter vivos, per stirpes* and *trustee* are only a few of the legal terms you'll run across when reading a trust document. Don't be intimidated by the Latin or legalese. This book will introduce you to the most important terms and define them for you. Every new term is followed, when necessary, by a plain-language explanation. You can also turn to the glossary (Appendix VI) for help as you proceed through the book. You'll find that a few key terms are used repeatedly, and that once you learn them you'll be well on your way to understanding how trusts work.

HOW TO USE THIS MANUAL

This book describes what trusts are, the different kinds that are available, why people use them and when you should consult a professional for advice or drafting.

Part I opens with a general discussion of trusts and some popular misconceptions about them. It then addresses the importance of avoiding or at least minimizing probate and explains which estate-planning tools are used with, or instead of, trusts.

Part II includes an explanation of the elements common to all types of trusts, how trusts affect taxes and what you need to know before selecting trustees and beneficiaries. The section ends with a chapter on where to get more information and help in drafting your own trust.

Parts III and IV discuss specific types of trusts: living trusts, testamentary (or will) trusts and special-purpose trusts. Such matters as how the various trusts are used, who uses them and who are typically named as beneficiaries are covered. For each type of trust, a list is provided of advantages and disadvantages—information you need before deciding which kind of trust, if any, is best for you.

Living trusts, in particular revocable living trusts, are dealt with in the greatest detail because of their popularity.

If you are drafting your own trust, you can use the sample language as a starting place.

The appendixes at the back of the book give additional material such as state-by-state information on the laws governing trusts, federal and state tax material, a worksheet, trust schedule, glossary and bibliography.

DEALING WITH PROFESSIONALS

Most people assume they must hire a lawyer to set up a trust. But as we will see in Chapter 8, you can consult a variety of professionals including lawyers, accountants, bank trust officers, insurance underwriters and financial planners. And even if you decide to hire a lawyer, it may be possible—particularly in the case of an estate valued at under $600,000—to save money by doing some of the preliminary work yourself. As you get more deeply into this book, you will learn how to evaluate what services you need as well as how to approach the work that needs to be done.

The important thing is to know *all* your options before you look for professional help: You'll be rewarded with both financial savings and the knowledge that you are retaining control over your own legal affairs.

PART I

TRUSTS AND ESTATE PLANNING

CHAPTER 1

WHAT IS A TRUST?

A trust is a legal entity that can own, hold and pay out *assets* (money or property) that are given to it. Typically, you create a trust by drafting and signing a document that transfers legal *title* to designated property to the trust. After holding the assets for a specified time, the trust pays out the assets to those who are named, as instructed in the trust document. Most trusts involve a *grantor* (the person who creates the trust), a *trustee* (the person who manages the trust) and one or more *beneficiaries* (the people or groups who eventually benefit from the trust assets).

Because the law considers the trust a separate entity, any property you turn over to it belongs to the trust, not to you. The trust simply continues to manage your property as you've instructed it to. Depending on how the trust is set up, the assets in the trust can be exempt from taxes or probate—or both.

The term "trust" is generic, much like the term "vehicle." Just as you might select from among many types of vehicles (a car, a van, a bus, a motorcycle) to satisfy specific needs or conditions, you also have a choice among types of trusts, depending on your needs. For example, trusts are classified by:

- Whether they can be changed or canceled *(revocability)*
- Whether they take effect while you are alive or only after you die *(living* or *testamentary)*

- Who the *beneficiary* is (a private individual or charitable organization)

Trusts are also classified by purpose—what they're supposed to do. Generally they fall into broad categories, for example: *marital, support, charitable* and *insurance* trusts. Although these groupings do not cover all types of trusts or every purpose a trust might serve and are not mutually exclusive from one another (for example, a marital trust provides financial support for a surviving spouse), they do cover most estate-planning trusts.

Marital trusts are created by married couples with the primary goal of maximizing the tax advantages of the IRS's marital-deduction rules. Spouses who have combined estates worth more than $600,000 can take advantage of some common marital trusts, such as the POA and QTIP trusts. Both are discussed in Chapter 13.

Support trusts allow you to control how much property the beneficiary will receive and when. You might, for example, set up a support trust to provide a family member with a regular income, or to fund a child's future education. Many "living trusts" are support trusts. Living trusts are discussed in Chapters 9 and 10 and support trusts for children in Chapter 14.

Charitable trusts are established to contribute to a charity—such as the local zoo, the American Cancer Society or a university. Because they benefit the general public, such trusts get special tax treatment. The details of charitable trusts are found in Chapter 16.

Insurance trusts, not surprisingly, hold the proceeds from insurance policies—most often life insurance. People whose assets exceed $600,000 including their life insurance proceeds can use this kind of trust to minimize the federal estate tax bite. Such a trust can also give them control over when, how much of and to whom the proceeds will be released while avoiding probate. Chapter 15 discusses insurance trusts.

MISCONCEPTIONS ABOUT TRUSTS

Trusts Are Only for the Rich

It may have been true years ago that only rich people put their money and property into trusts, but that is no longer the case. The rich still use trusts to pass along their wealth and obtain tax breaks, but so do more and more people of middle income.

Partly thanks to Norman Dacey, the author of the best-selling *How to Avoid Probate!,* many people have learned that trusts offer advantages for "average" folks who want to pass their modest assets on to their children or other heirs without major problems, delays or payments for taxes, lawyers' fees and other legal expenses. So even if you're not wealthy, you can benefit from setting up a trust.

You Won't Have to Pay Taxes

Whether you pay taxes or not depends on the type of trust you set up and how much control over its property you retain. For example, a revocable living trust (one you can change or cancel at any time) offers no real tax advantage. Because it is set up to provide you with income during your life, you have to pay income taxes on the money you receive—just as if you had no trust at all. And because you retain control over the trust assets, they are considered part of your estate for federal tax purposes. To gain any significant tax advantage, you must relinquish total control over all of the trust's property.

Further, setting up any kind of trust simply to avoid federal estate taxes is pointless unless you're worth more than $600,000. That is the present level at which federal estate taxes take effect. If you own less, you won't have to pay federal estate taxes, regardless of whether you put your assets in a trust or not.

You Can Use Trusts to Avoid Probate

Not always. Some trusts are created *in* wills. They're called *testamentary* (or *will*) trusts and do not take effect until you die and after your will is probated. (More on this legal process in the next chapter.) You can avoid probate, however, by setting up a living trust (see Chapters 9 and 10). Assets in the trust don't go through probate because legal title to the property is not in your name, but in the trust's.

You Can Use Trusts to Avoid
Paying Your Debts

While some people have successfully hidden their assets from creditors by using trusts, the trend in court is to make the creator of the trust pay if a creditor sues to collect on a bill. A judge may even decide that you don't deserve to receive some or any of the property placed in the trust if it's found that you intentionally tried to use a trust to avoid your debts.

Everyone Should Have a Trust

This is a recently propagated myth. Though trusts can offer substantial benefits, some people go through life never needing one; others don't need one until late in life, after they accumulate a substantial amount of property.

When you consider that the most common reason to set up a trust is to avoid probate, you probably wouldn't create one for that reason if:

• You qualify for simplified probate or are exempt from probate procedures because your net estate is worth less than the dollar limit set by the probate court. (In most states, that's between $10,000 and $60,000.)

- Your major assets would bypass probate anyway because they are co-owned with others who will inherit automatically.
- Your estate-planning needs are modest and met adequately by a will, a durable power of attorney for health care and a living will.

If You Have a Trust, You Don't Need a Will

Wrong. You should have a will even if you've put *all* your assets into a trust set up deliberately to distribute your property outside of probate. A will can ensure that assets not covered in your trust document (a last-minute inheritance or money won in a lottery or lawsuit) get into the trust (see Chapter 11). Finally, a will can take care of such other matters as naming a guardian for minor children.

Many of these issues are discussed more fully in the next two chapters, on probate and estate planning.

CHAPTER 2

WHY AVOID PROBATE?

Probate is the legal process a state imposes before allowing transfer of most of a deceased person's property to the heirs. If someone dies leaving a will, the court's first order of business is to approve the will (virtually automatic unless the will is challenged) and the executor or personal representative (PR) named in it and to make sure all property owned by the person who died is accounted for and distributed according to the will's instructions. A person who dies without a will is said to die intestate; in that case, the court will appoint a PR (usually a member of the decedent's family) to oversee distribution of the estate according to the state's intestacy laws. (Intestacy laws vary from state to state; they spell out what percentage family members will receive of a deceased person's estate if that person dies without a will or other provision. Under intestacy laws, your estate might be distributed in a way that is different from what you would have liked.)

Probate sounds simple enough, and in practice it should be.

Why, then, do people talk about avoiding it like the plague? Two reasons: time and money. Probate can use too much of both. The process can take up to a year or more, and legal fees can run as high as 10 percent of the estate's value, regardless of how much time or work was needed. If a lawyer has been named PR in the will or by the court, there may be no way of avoiding most of these fees.

Sometimes you don't even have to die before the probate system closes in on your property. Ethel F. Donahue, an 88-year-old Connecticut resident with considerable assets—$38 million—suffered several small strokes in 1979. Judge James H. Kinsella of Hartford ruled that she was incapable of handling her own affairs and named two close attorney friends to supervise her estate, along with a third attorney.

The three lawyers wrangled over control of the estate, the largest ever handled by the court. By the time the wrangling stopped, they had amassed more than $500,000 in fees—all without the knowledge of Donahue, her friends or her relatives. The case hit the newspapers, and lengthy legal maneuvering and investigations resulted in the judge's resignation on the eve of impeachment hearings and formal discipline against the lawyers.

PROBATE COSTS

Newspaper headlines like "Legal Fees Eat Up Half of Estate" or "Probate Fees Legalized Racket" are scary but not uncommon. What should you expect to pay? The answer depends on the value of your estate and:

- Whether a lawyer is the PR or hired by the PR to help settle the estate
- What estate-planning tools were used to transfer the assets
- What type of probate administration is required

Has a Lawyer Been Appointed PR or Hired by the PR?

If you want to keep probate costs down, it is a good idea *not* to name a lawyer as PR of your will. Most lawyers can and will charge handsomely for their PR services. They'll collect either a percentage of the estate's value or a "reasonable" fee.

Percentage Fee   In states that use the percentage-fee system, the maximum a lawyer or other PR can charge is based on the estate's value. For example, an attorney may be allowed to charge up to 10 percent of the first $20,000 of an estate's value and 4 percent of the remaining value. Some states even allow a lawyer–PR to collect twice from the same estate—one percentage fee for serving as PR, another for serving as the estate's legal counsel.

Sometimes the court may allow your PR to include the value of your jointly owned home when calculating fees, even though ownership of your home bypasses probate and goes directly to the surviving owner. However, courts will *not* allow property you put into a living trust to be included in the value of your estate when calculating the percentage fee, because the property is owned by the trust, not by you.

Reasonable Fee   Some states have replaced percentage fees with what are called "reasonable" fees. These are intended to modify the effects of percentage fees by basing charges on the actual work done, the time and skill required, and the customary amount charged for probate in the local community. Although this is an improvement, a review of probate fees charged in states that apply criteria of reasonability reveals that many lawyers still base their bills on the size of the estate, not on the complexity of the work they did. On the positive side, in these states heirs at least have an opportunity to challenge fee requests as unreasonable, a right not available in the percentage-fee system.

To keep probate costs down, it's much better to appoint as your PR someone who is unlikely to charge a fee or who will only ask a nominal amount, such as a family member or trusted friend. A PR who needs legal advice should know in advance that laws regulating probate fees dictate only what lawyers are *allowed* to charge, not what they're *required* to charge. Armed with that information, the PR can shop for a lawyer who will charge by the hour and only for work actually done.

Have Other Estate-Planning Tools Been Used?

You can transfer property directly to your surviving spouse, friends or other relatives in any of several ways that avoid the trouble, delay and expense of probate. These options are discussed in greater detail in Chapter 3 and the chapters on living trusts. It's sufficient here to suggest only a few of the more commonly used strategies: living trusts, joint tenancy with the right of survivorship, and designation of a beneficiary on your life insurance policy or retirement fund. In *none* of these cases will the property involved be considered part of your probate estate. If you appoint a nonlawyer PR, the chances are much improved that such property will also not be included in the value of your estate when calculating probate fees.

What Type of Probate Administration Is Required?

Probate procedures can be time consuming and expensive or relatively quick and inexpensive, depending on several factors. Three basic types of proceedings are used for probating an estate: supervised, unsupervised, and small-estate administration.

Supervised administration involves direct court supervision of all or parts of the process; this is the norm and is the probate process most people try to avoid. By contrast, *unsupervised* administration has little court supervision and few formal reporting requirements. *Small-estate administration* procedures, which involve almost no formalities, are used for estates valued at less than specified dollar limits set by state law.

Which process your estate will require depends on your

state's laws, the value of the estate being probated and whether you die with or without a will. The desirability of using the simpler procedures is a further reason for being sure you have a will and that your estate plan transfers as much of your property as possible outside of probate. Unsupervised probate will involve far less paperwork and fewer trips to the courthouse.

PROBATE DELAYS

The probate process can consume a few months to several years, although most estates are settled and distributed in about 18 months.

Some delays are built into the system deliberately to protect distant or out-of-contact heirs or creditors who may want to file claims against the estate. Some delays may not be necessary, however. According to a 1990 report by the American Association of Retired Persons, "A Report on Probate: Consumer Perspectives and Concerns," few creditors use the probate system to collect debts. Instead, most collect directly from the survivors.

European nations certainly don't think probate needs to be such a lengthy and cumbersome process. In England, estates are probated and assets distributed within three weeks of a person's death. In Germany, it takes only 36 hours. In the United States, however, you can do little to avoid the delay beyond appointing a trustworthy and efficient PR and using estate-planning tools—such as a living trust—that allow as much of your assets as possible to bypass probate entirely.

WHERE TO FIND OUT MORE

For more information on probate, obtain a copy of *Probate: Settling an Estate** or check the titles listed in Appendix VII. Also, call the probate court clerk or registrar and ask if you can get a plain-language guide to your state's or county's probate system. Finally, check with local consumer affairs offices and your state's attorney general's office to see if any such guides are available to the public.

*This step-by-step guide, which takes you through the probate process, was written by Kay Ostberg in association with HALT, Random House, 1990.

CHAPTER 3

ESTATE-PLANNING TOOLS

Although more and more people are using trusts to avoid probate and to pass their property on to heirs, there are also other estate-planning tools that may meet your needs better than a trust can or that can be used in combination with a trust.

These devices include:

- Naming beneficiaries on insurance or retirement fund registration forms
- Setting up a joint tenancy with right of survivorship on ownership documents, whether a bank account registration or the deed to real estate
- Making outright gifts of property to your heirs while you're still alive
- Writing a will

The first three allow you to pass your property directly to others outside of probate, a major goal of estate planning. (A will, of course, must be probated.) For more information on estate-planning strategies, refer to the books listed in Appendix VII.

NAMING A BENEFICIARY

Most retirement funds and all life insurance proceeds can be transferred directly to your beneficiaries without going through probate. If you want more flexibility over when and in what amounts your beneficiaries receive these funds, you can transfer the assets to a *living trust* (see Chapters 9 and 10) or *testamentary trust* (see Chapter 12) by naming the trust as beneficiary. Then spell out in the trust how you want the benefits to be paid out. As we will see, however, if you choose to pass these benefits on to a testamentary trust, they'll have to be probated.

Individual Retirement Accounts (IRAs)

An Individual Retirement Account (IRA) is a special savings plan under which you can designate your beneficiary on the account registration document. When you die, any funds still in the IRA will pass directly to the beneficiary you designated. The funds won't have to go through probate unless you do not name a beneficiary, you name your estate as the beneficiary, or your beneficiary dies before you do.

Under IRS rules, you can deposit up to $2,000 each year in your IRA. (The money you deposit may or may not be taxed in the year you earned it, depending on whether you or your spouse are covered by a qualified retirement plan or your combined income exceeds certain IRS levels.) As you withdraw the funds, you will have to pay income tax on any previously untaxed amounts. For most people, this will be at a lower rate than they would have paid when they first earned the money, because lower retirement income can be expected to put them in a lower tax bracket.

Keoghs

A "Keogh" is a retirement plan available only to the self-employed. As with IRAs, if your Keogh account still contains money when you die, those funds will be released to the beneficiary you named on the account. If you do not name a beneficiary, if you name your estate as beneficiary or if the beneficiary dies before you do, the money will be released to your estate and will go through probate.

As with IRAs, you can defer paying income taxes on your investments until you withdraw money from the account, presumably when you are in a lower tax bracket. The biggest advantage of a Keogh is that depending on the type of plan you create, you can invest up to $30,000 or 25 percent of your income, whichever is less.

Employer Pension Plans

If you are covered by a pension plan where you work, the benefits will generally be paid your surviving spouse when you die and will not have to go through probate. Few pension plans pay benefits to anyone other than a spouse.

Life Insurance

According to the American Council of Life Insurance, 9 of every 10 families in the United States have some form of life insurance, typically term or whole life. ("Term" insurance covers you for a specific period and must be renewed for coverage to continue; you may not borrow against it. "Whole life" covers you until you die; you may cash it in for its accumulated value or leave the entire amount for your beneficiary to collect.)

People buy life insurance primarily to protect those economically dependent on them—a spouse, child, elderly parent or sibling. If you have such insurance and designate a beneficiary on the policy, when you die the company will pay the proceeds directly to that beneficiary. They will be exempt from probate, but the money will be considered part of your taxable estate. If the insurance payment will dramatically increase the value of your estate, you can place the policy in an insurance trust (see Chapter 15).

JOINT TENANCY WITH RIGHT OF SURVIVORSHIP

A joint tenancy with right of survivorship is an easy and inexpensive way for both married and unmarried people to own property. Each owner holds equal interest in the entire piece of property—whether it's a checking account, a residence or a savings bond. When one of them dies, that owner's share automatically transfers to the co-owner (or co-owners) without passing through probate.

You may not leave your joint-tenancy rights to another person in a will or testamentary trust: The surviving joint tenant gets your share when you die. To create a joint tenancy with automatic right of survivorship, it's best to put the survivorship clause in writing; in fact, some states require it. There's nothing complicated about this: Simply write the words "Joint tenants with right of survivorship" after your names on the account registration or other ownership document.

Most estate-planning professionals feel that joint tenancy is an excellent arrangement for spouses or for those who agree on the disposal of the property after they die. Co-owning property with someone who has different ideas about how long your relationship as co-owners will last, or who should inherit the property, can throw a wrench into your estate plans. Also, while it's true that you'll avoid probate by using a joint tenancy with right of survivorship, when the last surviving joint tenant dies, the property will have to go through probate. One way for married couples to get around this is to place their jointly held assets into a living trust (see Chapters 9 and 10).

OUTRIGHT GIFTS

If your estate is worth more than $600,000, your heirs will probably have to pay a federal estate tax. You can reduce the size of your taxable estate by giving some of your money or other assets to your intended heirs while you're still alive. This is a common strategy for those who know years before they die whom they intend to give their assets to.

Under the annual gift tax exclusion law, an individual can give up to $10,000 a year, or a husband and wife can together make a gift of up to $20,000 a year, to each of any number of people, tax free. The recipient (for example, your friend, relative or anyone else you have in mind) must have an immediate right to the gift, however; it cannot be tied to some future event, such as reaching a specified age.

If, instead, you want to give the gift with "strings attached," you can place it in an irrevocable living trust, thereby reducing the size of your taxable estate. You must write into the trust document your instructions about when the money can be released (see Chapter 10 for details of irrevocable living trusts).

WILLS

A will is the most common estate-planning tool, other than the self-transferring methods discussed above. Any property transferred by will, however, *must* go through probate.

A will, of course, tells the state and your family exactly whom you want to inherit your property. It also allows you to name a guardian for minor children or other dependents; to give special instructions, such as for funeral arrangements; and to make specific bequests and requests. The person you appoint in your will to carry out your wishes is called the executor or, for females, the executrix.

As noted earlier, if you die without a will *and* without taking advantage of any of the probate-avoidance techniques discussed above, your state will decide, according to its distribution guidelines, which of your relatives will inherit your property. Unless that doesn't matter to you, it is far better to leave a will than to die without one. For tips on how to find help in drafting your will, see Chapter 8.

PART II

CREATING
A TRUST

CHAPTER 4

TRUST BASICS

This chapter seeks to give basic information about what trusts are, what they do and what elements they have in common.

A FLEXIBLE TOOL

As we have noted, a trust is a legal device that allows one or more persons to hold legal title to and manage property for the benefit of others. That generic description doesn't, however, convey the true power and practicality of trusts.

Trusts can give you considerably more flexibility in exercising control over your property than any other estate-planning tool. As the person who sets up the trust, you get to decide how long that trust will hold your property, how the trust assets will be managed and invested, and how and when assets will be disposed of. You can even reserve the right to change your mind or cancel the trust altogether.

For example: You may run a family business and worry about what would happen to it if you were to die before your children could take over. By placing the business into a living trust, you can be assured that when you die, your business will not have to go through probate, it will not be sold to pay off debts and it can continue operating. Without a trust, you can be sure of none of those things.

Your trust can also accommodate changing contingencies. For example, you can list in the trust document the backup people you want to have step in if your children decide they have other career plans in mind, or if after you die the person you choose to run the business also dies before your children can take over.

THE PURPOSES OF A TRUST

Preserving a family business is only one of many reasons for setting up a trust. Actually, you can set up a trust for *any* purpose, as long as it's legal.

The most common reason for setting up a trust is to make sure its assets are managed, conserved and distributed as you want and to whom you want. More specifically, you can have your trust:

- Reduce or avoid taxes
- Avoid the trouble, expense and delay of probate
- Ensure that your financial and personal affairs will be taken care of the way you want if you become incapacitated
- Provide financial support for a dependent spouse or children after you die
- Protect your property from a fiscally irresponsible beneficiary
- Provide financial support for a mentally or physically disabled dependent
- Ensure that your property is passed along bloodlines (for example, to your son but not to his wife)
- Protect your children from receiving an inheritance before they are old enough to manage it
- Ensure that your business is managed the way you want
- Make alimony payments
- Finance your child's education

- Determine when, how and to whom your life insurance will be paid
- Support a charitable organization

THE "PARTIES"

A trust involves up to three people or groups of people: the one who creates the trust and supplies the assets for it *(grantor);* the one who holds legal title to the property and manages it *(trustee);* and the one who will benefit from the trust *(beneficiary).*

In a few instances, the same person may play all three roles; see, for example, the discussion of charitable remainder trusts in Chapter 16. More common, however, are trust agreements that involve two or more people. In fact, with most trusts, if only one person is involved and that person acts as both the sole trustee and sole beneficiary, the law may say a "merger" has occurred and may rule that a trust doesn't exist. Why? Because a trust is supposed to separate an interest in property into a *legal interest* and a *beneficial interest.* (The distinction between the two is explained below.) If only one person enjoys both the legal and beneficial interests in the trust property, then no separation has occurred. The way to avoid this is to involve two or more people in the trust. The role of each is reviewed briefly below.

The Grantor   This person or group creates the trust and supplies it with property or assets. Other names for the grantor are *settlor, maker, donor* or *trustor.*

As a grantor, all you need to create a trust is property (cash or other assets) to put into it and legal authority to give *(convey)* the property to someone else. You may not have that legal authority if the law considers you "legally incompetent" to do so. You are probably not considered legally competent, for example, if you are a minor (usually under age 18), mentally unstable or bankrupt. "Incompetents" may not be grantors or trustees, but they can be—and often are—named as beneficiaries.

In the trust document, the grantor gives the trustee a legal interest in the property and gives the beneficiary an equitable or beneficial interest in it. *Legal interest* simply means the right to control the investment and distribute the property as directed by the trust. *Beneficial interest* is simply the law's way of describing the right to enjoy and use the trust property (either the principal or interest) as the trust stipulates.

The Trustee   This is the person or institution named by the grantor to hold legal title to the trust assets and manage them. In most states, any person or entity capable of taking legal title—including individuals, corporations and government agencies—may be appointed trustee. It is common for grantors of living trusts to name themselves as trustees so they can maintain complete control over the trust's assets.

Trustees have a legal, fiduciary duty to protect the trust's assets and see to it that the purposes of the trust are served. The duties and responsibilities of the trustee are discussed in detail in Chapter 6. The powers given to the trustee to carry out these duties are spelled out by the grantor in the trust document. They can be anything from complex arrangements and schedules of payments to statements as simple as "disburse all property to my daughter Chantal upon my death" or "use your personal judgment about when and how much of the trust income Chantal will get until she's twenty-five, then disburse all remaining property to her."

Successor Trustee   Every trust should also designate someone to take over if the original trustee dies or is otherwise unable to manage the trust. If you do not appoint a successor trustee, the court has authority to do so if one is needed.

In a living trust, where spouses typically are cotrustees, the successor trustee would take over only if both spouses die.

The Beneficiary   The trust is created to give property to a beneficiary. This can be a person or any institution, whether it's a for-profit corporation or a charity. The beneficiary may be an *income beneficiary* assigned earnings from the trust, such as interest from a savings account, or a *principal beneficiary,* to receive the actual assets—for example, the money in the savings account. Or a beneficiary might receive both income and principal, either at the discretion of the trustee or in specified amounts.

Grantors also often name alternate beneficiaries to receive the trust property if the primary beneficiary cannot, for whatever reason, and a *residual beneficiary,* who takes what's left of the trust property when the trust ends.

THE ELEMENTS OF EVERY TRUST

A trust should be established in a written document that is clear and specific. It should include the following basic elements.

Intent to Create a Trust

Every trust must state clearly—either in writing, orally or by conduct—that you intend to create a trust. Although no special or "legal" words have to be used, uncertain or ambiguous terms certainly could invalidate your trust. Be as specific as you can in identifying your intention, the parties to the trust, the property you're putting into it and the purpose of the trust.

The best way to do this is simply to state your intentions in writing. Some trusts must be in writing to comply with state laws encompassing the *Statute of Frauds;* trusts that involve land or other real estate, for example, must always be in writing (see Appendix I for your state's requirements). Regardless of whether your state's laws require a trust to be in writing, it is the best way to ensure that your intentions are clear and permanently recorded. Also, there's little chance that a bank, insurance company, land registry or the like would recognize any transfer of your assets to a trust unless it can protect itself from future claims by having a copy of a written trust agreement in its own files.

The Trust Assets

Every trust must have assets. As grantor, you must designate what those assets are. The assets placed into a trust are referred to as *principal, subject matter, corpus, trust property* or *res.* They often include mortgages, titles to a house and/or land, bank accounts, bonds, stocks, cash and "interests" (such as future rent collections), insurance proceeds, the family business, or rights to a patent, copyright or trademark.

These assets must be described as specifically as possible if you want to avoid problems down the road. Stating that you want your sister to get "one of my cars" is, of course, not specific. Nor is leaving "my bank account to my brother" if you have several accounts.

The Trust Parties

Practically speaking, all three parties—grantor, trustee and beneficiary—must be identified in a way that makes it absolutely clear who they are. You shouldn't identify the beneficiary as your "spouse" or even "Mrs. James Flatley." Think of the confusion if you married more than once! Instead, use a person's full legal name plus an identifier, such as an address or Social Security number: "Elizabeth M. Flatley, of 17 Monroe Lane, Small Town, MA."

If you fail to name a trustee, the court will appoint one; a trust is never found invalid because its trustee is not named.

The same isn't true for beneficiaries, however: if you don't name a beneficiary, the courts say you don't have a trust. In fact, courts have found trusts valid when the beneficiary was the *only* party identified.

A Valid Purpose

A trust may be created for any purpose that does not violate the law or public policy. The variety of valid purposes for which trusts are created was discussed earlier in this chapter. Some illegal and invalid purposes include defrauding creditors, depriving a spouse of marital rights and encouraging questionable behavior, such as sexual relations, with a beneficiary. If you want to make your trust contingent on any such conditions, expect to have it declared invalid.

DISTRIBUTING THE ASSETS

When you set up a trust, you decide how much will be paid to your named beneficiaries and when, as well as how the trustee is to carry out any other assigned duties.

As with any investment, the assets are either the principal or the income generated by the principal. You can direct a trustee to pay out only the trust's income or to "invade" or distribute the principal as well. Any of the following distribution plans can be used with any trust.

Lump-Sum Distribution Under this arrangement, income from the principal is allowed to accumulate, either passively or through aggressive reinvestment schemes, instead of being paid out. Only after a designated triggering event—a wedding, a graduation, a specified date or even the trust assets' accumulating to a specified dollar value—are the income and principal paid to the beneficiary.

Trusts that provide for lump-sum distribution are often called "accumulation trusts." States have laws that restrict how long trust funds can accumulate. If you're interested in setting up this type of trust, you should find out about the applicable state laws (see "Rule Against Perpetuities" in this chapter and Appendix I).

Periodic Distribution Trust income or principal may also be paid out at scheduled intervals—for example, weekly, monthly or quarterly. The payments, in effect, provide the beneficiary with a regular income.

Periodic distributions are typically used in support trusts for minor children, a dependent spouse or a financially incompetent individual. Often, the trust specifies that the funds cannot be used for anything other than designated support—such as food, clothing, shelter and education—and therefore cannot be touched by a beneficiary's creditors (unless the creditor provided the necessity; see Appendix I). Support trusts can be either living or testamentary—that is, created to go into effect in your lifetime (even if payments from the fund aren't to begin until after you die) or written into your will to be funded and to go into effect when you die.

Discretionary or "Sprinkle" Distribution Under this arrangement, the trustee has discretion to "sprinkle" money where and when it's most needed—for example, giving an unemployed child twice as much each month as an employed child. Typically, the trustee has complete control over how much will be paid out and when and is not limited to making distributions for support alone.

When Beneficiaries Die Before You Do

If a lawyer drafts your trust, or if you use a preprinted trust form, chances are that you will see either the words *per stirpes* or *per capita* in the clause specifying how the assets are to be distributed. These words are important because they describe how your assets will be passed to your descendants if any of your immediate beneficiaries die before you do. If the phrase *per stirpes* is used, it means that your grandchildren inherit equal shares of the property that their parent (your child) would have inherited had he or she lived. If the phrase *per capita* is used, it means that all beneficiaries involved (actually all of your living descendants, regardless of generation) get equal shares of your estate.

How Money Is Disbursed under *Per Stirpes* Under a *per stirpes* distribution plan, if one of your beneficiaries dies before you do, the amount that beneficiary would have received had he or she lived will be passed on to the beneficiary's direct descendants.

In the example below, Jill would have inherited one third of her mother's estate—just like her brothers, John and Josh.

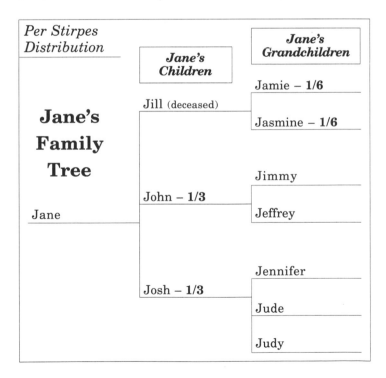

Per Stirpes Distribution	*Jane's Children*	*Jane's Grandchildren*
Jane's Family Tree	Jill (deceased)	Jamie – 1/6
		Jasmine – 1/6
	John – 1/3	Jimmy
Jane		Jeffrey
	Josh – 1/3	Jennifer
		Jude
		Judy

Since Jill died before her mother, Jill's children will inherit Jill's third after their grandmother dies. They will split the third between them.

How Money Is Disbursed under *Per Capita*   Under a *per capita* distribution plan, if one of your beneficiaries dies before you do, all of your remaining living descendants (all children, grandchildren, great-grandchildren, etc.) could inherit equal shares of your estate.

In the example below, since there are nine living descendants, each would inherit one ninth of Jane's estate. If Jane wanted only her surviving children to inherit her estate, her trust should state, "in equal shares to my children surviving at my death, per capita and not per stirpes."

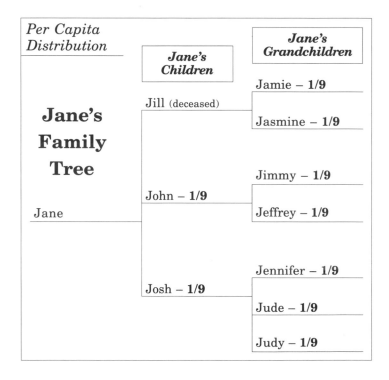

Per Capita Distribution

Jane's Family Tree

Jane

Jane's Children

Jill (deceased)

John – **1/9**

Josh – **1/9**

Jane's Grandchildren

Jamie – **1/9**

Jasmine – **1/9**

Jimmy – **1/9**

Jeffrey – **1/9**

Jennifer – **1/9**

Jude – **1/9**

Judy – **1/9**

THE MAJOR CATEGORIES

Trusts are most commonly classified as:

- *Testamentary* or *living*
- *Revocable* or *irrevocable*

Each has probate and tax implications, and each has characteristics that determine how much control over the assets you retain or give up.

Testamentary or Living

Testamentary trusts (sometimes called *court* or *will* trusts) are created in a person's will and take effect only when that person dies.

The most obvious shortcoming of these trusts is that they must go through probate.

A testamentary trust does have some advantages, however. It can be used to minimize taxes, changed at any time until you die, and allow you to control how your estate is managed and distributed after you die.

It can also protect a beneficiary's inheritance from some of life's mishaps. For example, if your son divorces, he won't have to share your estate with his ex-wife. And if you want the probate court to look over your trustee's shoulder and aren't concerned about the cost attached to that supervision, then a testamentary trust could be the thing for you (see Chapter 12).

Living (or *inter vivos*) trusts take effect during your lifetime. They are created not in your will but in a document separate from your will. Most people who set up living trusts appoint themselves (and, if married, their spouse) as trustee and income beneficiary. That allows them to manage the trust and to be paid by it on a schedule they themselves establish. After they die, the remaining income and principal go to the beneficiaries they designate in the trust. This arrangement does not violate the "merger" issue discussed on page 25 because someone other than the person(s) who set up the trust ultimately benefits from it.

Typically, if a married couple creates a living trust and one of them dies, the surviving spouse continues to serve as trustee and continues to receive income from the trust for life. After both spouses die, their successor trustee (named in the trust or by the court) steps in to keep the trust going or to disburse the trust's assets to the beneficiaries.

The major benefit of a living trust is that the property you place into it is not considered part of your probate estate and therefore bypasses probate.

Revocable or Irrevocable

Living trusts can be either revocable or irrevocable. An *irrevocable trust* cannot be changed or canceled. A *revocable trust* can be changed or canceled *(revoked)* any time until the death or incompetency of the grantor. At the grantor's death or incompetency, it becomes irrevocable.

A grantor who wants to retain control over a living trust's property should expressly include a clause in the trust document stating that it is a revocable trust. If this clause is left out, a court may rule that the trust is irrevocable.

Anyone who sets up a living trust must decide whether to make it revocable. If you surrender control over your trust assets, you'll gain tax advantages. If you maintain control over your trust assets, you'll gain flexibility over the administration and disposition of those assets but lose the tax advantages. Determining which is more important to you—control or tax advantages—is one of the first decisions you have to make in creating a trust.

GOVERNING LAWS

Trusts have traditionally been governed by case law, but in recent years the states have adopted laws regulating various aspects of trust procedures (see Appendix I for a list of the states that have adopted one or more of these legislative acts).

Because living trusts are governed by state law, you can, theoretically, shop around and create your trust in the state that offers you the most advantages. For example, some states allow greater freedom in how you invest trust assets; others, but not all, allow *spendthrift clauses,* which protect the trust's assets from a beneficiary's creditors; still other states have lower income or estate taxes or no such taxes at all. Practically speaking, this doesn't happen very often. If you plan to create a trust out of state, seek professional help.

Testamentary trusts, which are written into wills, are governed by the laws of the state that govern the will—normally, the state in which you are living when you die.

Rule Against Perpetuities

This rule, which governs how long a trust can last, applies only to private, not to charitable, trusts. The rule prohibits an owner from controlling distribution of property from beyond the grave for too long. To prevent people, especially the wealthy, from creating trusts that tie up family property for generations, the rule states that a trust cannot own property for longer than the life of any living person named in the trust, plus 21 years. After such time, the interest in the property must *vest.* Within the time limit set by the rule, the beneficiary must receive full ownership rights to the property (not a *contingent interest*). If there's even a slight possibility that that won't happen, the trust violates the rule and is considered void from the beginning.

Few people need to worry about this rule, but if you are one of them, you should know that most states have adopted a "wait-and-see" approach: No trust is invalidated because of what might happen in those states. If a trust doesn't end up violating the rule (that is, if it ends within the time restrictions, as most do), it will be considered valid, even if its language made it possible that it would continue beyond the rule's limit.

Many trusts routinely include a clause to make sure the rule against perpetuities isn't violated. Here's some sample language:

> Any trust created herein that has not terminated sooner shall terminate twenty-one (21) years after the death of the last survivor of the class composed of [your name] and those of my children, grandchildren, and any of my more remote descendants who are living at my death.

Because many people have young grandchildren or young great-grandchildren when they die, the period of time produced by this clause averages around 90 years and in some cases can exceed 100 years. Be careful to note, however, that this clause does not state that the trust must last this long. It only states that the trust cannot last longer. Even though most trusts will terminate in a much shorter time, it is a good idea to put this clause in. The common-law rule is quirky, and without this clause it can invalidate a very reasonable trust. Also, the "wait-and-see" statutes, other than the Uniform Statutory Rule Against Perpetuities, are difficult to administer and can cause your heirs to go to court to find out what the statute means in your case. The use of the above clause avoids all these problems.

CHAPTER 5

TAXES

$\mathbf{A}$s we have seen, properly used, trusts can save you from paying taxes during your lifetime and also can protect your estate from taxes. This chapter will discuss the basic factors that must be considered to take advantage of these potential tax savings.

Sometimes it seems that as soon as tax specialists devise a new way to minimize taxes, the government comes up with a new rule to "close the tax loophole." Formerly popular trusts—the Clifford Trust, for example—are no longer attractive because IRS rules have eliminated their tax advantages.

Furthermore, as noted previously, an estate must amount to $600,000 or more for federal estate taxes (also called federal death taxes) to take effect. This figure includes any life insurance benefits but is computed after the deduction of charitable gifts, property passed on to a spouse and other allowable deductions. Various states do tax estates of much lower value but at a much lower rate than the federal government does (see below and also Appendix III).

Because of these and other complications, it is important to understand the basic trust options that are currently available.

Basically, trusts are used to lower three kinds of taxes: income taxes; federal estate and gift taxes; and state-imposed estate and gift taxes. This chapter examines ways to eliminate or reduce such taxes. If your situation is fairly complicated or if your estate is large, you should consult a tax expert for information about the latest tax laws and trust options.

LOWERING INCOME TAXES

Years ago, a surefire way to lower federal taxes on income from assets was to put those assets into an irrevocable trust. Any interest, rents or other income accumulated in the trust, and no tax had to be paid until the income was passed on to the beneficiaries.

Times have changed. Now, your trust pays federal income tax at a high rate, probably the same rate that you would have to pay on this income if you didn't have a trust. That's why people no longer create trusts to lower the income tax they have to pay on income produced by their assets— rental property, for instance, or stocks, bonds, savings certificates and other investments.

Trusts were also used to shift income to children, who paid lower taxes because of their typically lower annual incomes. When the top federal income tax rates ranged to 50 percent and more, having income taxed at the lower end of the tax table could mean a considerable savings.

Congress foreclosed this practice for the most part in the Tax Reform Act of 1986 by establishing the so-called kiddie tax. In effect, the IRS now treats all family income alike. Any investment income, including trust income, of more than $1,000 to any child less than 14 years old is taxed at the parents' tax rate, regardless of the source of income. To shift your income to a lower tax rate, it must go to a child of 14 or older who is in a lower tax bracket than you.

There is, however, still one trust that does provide you with income tax savings: the charitable trust. Your contributions to such a trust will be deductible on your federal income tax returns, within limits. Also, you normally do not have to pay taxes on any amount the donated property increased in value after it was purchased. Chapter 16 contains a more detailed explanation of the income tax advantages of charitable trusts.

With this one exception, creating an irrevocable trust with valuable property can actually *increase* the income taxes you or your heirs will eventually owe. If you have property that has increased substantially in value or is likely to do so, it is usually better to pass that property on to your heirs after you die than to put it into an irrevocable trust. When the trust sells the property, it will have to pay income taxes on the amount of increased value based on your original cost, just as you would if you had kept it and transferred it to someone else and banked the profit. The way to get around this is by using a revocable trust or by transferring the property in your will after you die. If the property is in a revocable trust or is transferred after you die, the taxes on the increased value are, in effect, forgiven.

EXAMPLE

Sam purchased a painting for $55,000 that is now valued at $755,000. He is thinking of putting it into a trust for his daughter, Wendy, so its value will not be included in his taxable estate. Sam decides on an irrevocable trust that will keep the assets he places in it out of his taxable estate. However, he discovers that when he puts the painting into a trust and the trust later sells it, the trust will have to pay income taxes on the $700,000 it increased in value after he bought it. If, instead, he leaves the painting to Wendy in his will, Wendy will inherit the value of the painting at what is called a "stepped-up basis"—what it's worth when Sam dies, presumably at least $755,000. Wendy will have to pay income taxes only on any increase in value beyond that amount, if and when she sells the painting. Sam calculates the federal and state income tax bite on $700,000, then the likely probate and estate taxes that would have to be paid if he includes the painting in his will. He decides the income tax bite is the greater evil and places other assets in the trust instead.

Before creating a trust with income-producing property, you should also determine who will owe the income taxes: you as the grantor or creator, the trust itself, or its beneficiaries. Like so much else in this field, it depends on what kind of trust you set up.

The basic rule is that whoever controls the income owes the taxes.

Revocable trusts have no current tax advantage. To lower current taxes you must give up ownership—that is, control—of your property. To put it another way, only irrevocable trusts save on income taxes.

If you, as the creator, retain the right to revoke the trust, or if you name yourself as beneficiary or as trustee with the right to manage the trust assets, then the trust's income is yours for tax purposes. It's considered a *grantor trust:* You pay taxes on its income, lumped in with your other income and taxed at the same rate. You still must file a separate tax form for the trust, but it's only an information return that says that you reported any income you receive from the trust on your regular tax forms. If, on the other hand, you *don't* retain the right to revoke the trust and *don't* name yourself either a beneficiary or trustee, the trust is considered to earn the income. It must file its own income tax returns and pay its own taxes. Any trust income that is given to a beneficiary is taxed once: The beneficiary pays the tax and, if he or she is age 14 or over, the income is included with his or her income to determine the tax rate.

FEDERAL ESTATE AND GIFT TAXES

If your estate is worth more than $600,000, depending on its total value, it will be subject to federal taxes of 37 to 55 percent.

EXAMPLE

Sally's taxable estate is worth $2 million. She leaves $1 million to her husband and the rest to her son, Daniel. No federal tax is owed on the money left to her husband—the unlimited marital deduction—and $600,000 of the $1 million she leaves to Daniel is exempt from tax. Federal estate tax will have to be paid on the remaining $400,000.

Any gifts you make during your lifetime that are over $10,000 each will not be exempt from taxes. Under the Unified Federal Estate and Gift Tax law, such gifts and wealth transferred after death are taxed at the same rate; the tax is calculated after you die. This is to prevent people from simply giving away their property before they die to escape the federal estate tax.

After you die, any gift you made during your lifetime that amounted to more than $10,000 to any individual during any year lowers your federal estate tax exemption by the excess amount you gave away. You may make gifts of $10,000 a year to each of as many people as you like without incurring taxes (you need not even file a gift tax return for these gifts), but you do have to file a return, IRS Form 709, if you give more than $10,000 to any person. Any amounts greater than the $10,000 exclusion per person are subtracted from your $600,000 exemption. In some states, you might even have to pay a state tax on large gifts (see "State Gift Tax," below).

EXAMPLE

Christopher gave $50,000 a year to his son and daughter-in-law each year for three years. He left his total remaining estate, worth $1 million at his death, to the same son and daughter-in-law. Because Christopher gave them more than $20,000 a year (that is, more than $10,000 to each of them each year), his estate will not get the full $600,000 federal tax exemption. Instead, he gets an exemption of only $510,000—the $600,000 reduced by the $90,000 he gave away ($30,000 a year for three years) that exceeded the annual gift allowance. At Christopher's death, federal taxes are owed on $490,000: the $1 million estate minus the $510,000 federal exemption remaining to him after subtracting the excess gifts.

Although this tax exemption is usually described as an "exemption," it's really a tax "credit." If the taxable estate is more than $600,000, whoever is administering the estate must file a federal estate tax form (IRS Form 706). On this form, the filer calculates the federal estate tax for the total value of the estate, not just the value above $600,000; the filer then subtracts, as a credit, the tax due on the first $600,000. The rest is the amount of tax that must be paid. If large gifts made during the deceased person's lifetime lower the exemption, the filer must add any excess gifts back to the taxable estate. In the example above, at Christopher's death, $90,000 is added back to the gross estate as "adjusted taxable gifts."

LOWERING THE FEDERAL ESTATE TAX

A 37 percent tax bite is no small matter, and that's the *lowest* rate that will have to be paid on any value of an estate above $600,000. To minimize what will be owed the government when you die, you can do the following.

Give Money to Your Spouse   Anything passed on to your spouse is free of estate tax. If you are a young, healthy couple, naming each other sole beneficiary makes tax sense. If the unexpected occurs and one of you dies, the other will have full access to the estate.

However, if you and your spouse are reasonably wealthy and retired or approaching retirement age, and if your children are grown with families of their own, this may not be the best plan. That's because if you pass everything you own on to your spouse, you may simply be bumping the value of your spouse's estate beyond the $600,000 federal exemption without benefiting from your own $600,000 exemption. The marital trusts described in Chapter 13 offer some of the devices you may use to take advantage of your own federal tax credit, lower the value of your spouse's eventual taxable estate and still give your spouse access to income from your assets (but not the principal) after you die.

Give Money to Charity Donations to charity are not included in your taxable estate. They are deducted from your gross estate.

Give $10,000 ($20,000 If You're a Married Couple) Each Year to Your Heirs If you know to whom you want to leave your money and can spare it now, you may give tax-free gifts of up to $10,000 to each heir every year and thereby reduce the value of your taxable estate.

Create a Trust for Your Grandchildren You may also create what's called a generation-skipping trust, discussed in detail in Chapter 14. Your own estate will still have to pay federal estate tax, but this kind of trust gives your children access to income from your assets (but not the principal) after you die. It also allows you to pass the first $1 million of your assets to your grandchildren without a second federal estate tax bite when your children die.

For more information about federal estate taxes, the federal marital deduction and federal gift tax, call your regional IRS office and ask for IRS Publication 448, "Federal Estate and Gift Taxes." You might also want to review IRS Form 706, the federal estate tax return, and the detailed booklet of instructions that accompanies it.

STATE TAXES

The IRS isn't the only government office that wants a piece of your wealth when you die. Every state also imposes a tax on transfers of a deceased person's property. The three types of such state assessments are *inheritance taxes, estate taxes* and *credit estate taxes.* In most instances, however, these state taxes result in only a minor bite from your estate.

Credit Estate Tax   Every state has what is known as a credit estate tax, in effect a federal tax rebate whose net effect is that you pay nothing more than the federal tax. (The amount of tax is the state tax credit the IRS will allow your heirs to deduct from the federal estate tax your estate owes. Like the federal tax, credit estate tax affects only estates worth more than $600,000. Because this tax never increases what your estate owes, it is not a consideration when setting up a trust or estate plan.)

Inheritance and Estate Taxes   Some states impose either an estate tax or an inheritance tax, but never both. The significant differences between the two are how the tax is calculated and who must pay it. Estate taxes are based on the size of the estate. Inheritance taxes are based on the relationship of the heir to the deceased person and the amount each heir inherits.

States with inheritance taxes usually tax what's left to spouses, children and grandchildren at a lower rate than what's passed on to brothers and sisters; other beneficiaries such as cousins or friends are taxed at a higher rate. Typically, an inheriting spouse might be taxed only 1 or 2 percent of the value inherited while an unrelated friend might have to pay as much as 20 percent.

Personal exemptions also apply to these inheritance taxes in many states. As with the tax rates themselves, these exemptions vary from state to state and according to the relationship of the heir to the deceased person. In Iowa, for example, each son and daughter gets the first $50,000 tax free, while in Montana, they would get the entire amount tax free.

Instead of taxing the inheritance, a few states tax the estate itself. As with the federal estate tax, this is a percentage of the value of the estate. The more valuable the estate, the higher the percentage. For this tax, the relationship of the heir to the deceased is irrelevant. Only one tax schedule and usually only one exemption apply across the board for the estate as a whole.

Taxes are owed to the state in which the deceased resided, so if you live part of the year in one state and part in another, you might want to establish residency in the state with the most favorable tax laws. You can compare these rates in Appendix III. It is unlikely that the possible savings would be enough to make it worth your while to move from one state to another, but if you already reside in more than one state, you may want to establish legal residency in the most favorable one by identifying that state as your permanent residence—the one in which you vote and own your home.

Bear one cautionary note in mind, however. If you put real estate—a vacation home, say—into a trust, the tax laws of the state where the property is located apply, *not* the laws of the state in which you reside.

STATE GIFT TAX

Seven states impose a state gift tax that uses the same rules and rates as the states' death taxes. They are Delaware, Louisiana, New York, North Carolina, South Carolina, Tennessee and Wisconsin. The only estate-planning implication is that you might consider moving from a state with high taxes to one with more favorable laws if you have an extremely large estate and want to start distributing it as gifts to your heirs during your lifetime.

COMPUTING YOUR TAXABLE ESTATE

What is your taxable estate for federal estate tax purposes? The basic rule is that your taxable estate includes everything you own, whether it is subject to probate or not, less deductions, expenses and gifts to charities. You need to calculate your taxable estate because if it's more than $600,000, your heirs will probably have to pay a significant part of it in taxes.

Determine Your Gross Estate

Compute the total value of all property owned at death. In addition to the obvious (your share of your home, bank accounts, stocks, businesses, furniture and the like), your gross estate also includes:

Trusts   The entire value of any revocable trust you create is included in your gross estate. Its value is what you own and control.

If you create an irrevocable living trust but keep some ownership rights, the value of those rights is also added to your estate. For example, if you retain the right to use income from trust property for life, the value of the property that generates the income is included. Even if you retain only the power to designate whether your son or daughter ultimately receives the interest in an irrevocable trust, you are considered to have enough ownership rights that the value of the trust assets is included in your estate.

If you are a beneficiary of a trust set up by someone else, the value of your interest in that trust can also be part of your estate.

Normally, if you receive payments from a trust created by someone else, are not the trustee and the trust goes to someone else when you die, the value of the trust is *not* included in your estate.

If you have a general *power-of-appointment trust,* which

gives you the right to dispose of the trust assets as you see fit, including to yourself, all the property in this trust is part of your estate. Power-of-appointment trusts are discussed in Chapters 13 and 17.

If you set up a trust that gives your spouse lifetime income, with the remainder eventually going to someone else, the value of the lifetime income is included in your taxable estate. This is the only notable exception to the unlimited marital deduction rule.

Intangible Property Property whose market value may be far from obvious, such as patent rights, is also part of your estate.

Life Insurance If you retain the power to change the policy or give that power away less than three years before you die, the value of the policy is included in your estate. If you take out life insurance on someone else and die before that person does, the cash value of the policy is included in your estate.

Subtract Deductions from the Gross Estate

To calculate whether your estate surpasses the federal estate tax threshold of $600,000 and, if it does, how much of it is taxable, subtract from it: all property you leave to your spouse; funeral and last-illness expenses; money you owe and uncollectible money that's owed to you; charitable bequests; probate fees and other fees and expenses for administering the estate.

Once you have determined your taxable estate, you can check your tax rate on the federal tax chart in Appendix II. However, remember that this tentative tax will be reduced by the tax credit you get for the $600,000 exemption (reduced by lifetime gifts) as well as other credits, such as those for any state death taxes or estate taxes already paid.

CHAPTER 6

TRUSTEES AND BENEFICIARIES

Choosing your trustees and beneficiaries should be done with care, and alternates *(successors)* should always be named. Most of this chapter is devoted to trustees—how to select them, what powers to give them and what payment they typically require for their services. The chapter concludes with a brief discussion of beneficiaries: who is usually selected and how to identify them in your trust document.

SELECTING A TRUSTEE

The trustees you name should be responsible, business-minded and able to deal fairly with all of your trust's beneficiaries. You may name one trustee or several. Anyone is eligible who is not considered legally incompetent. Typically, people name as trustees:

- Themselves (in the case of living trusts)
- A spouse, sibling or parent
- A friend
- An institution, such as a bank or trust company

Most people choose one trustee or a married couple, plus an alternate. Because a trust is essentially an agreement between you—as grantor—and the trustee, it makes sense to get the trustee's permission in advance. Otherwise, if the trustee declines to serve, you will have to amend the trust document to choose another, let your alternate serve or, if you named several trustees, let those remaining handle the responsibilities.

If your trustee dies or has to be replaced for whatever reason, your alternate trustee will step in. If you didn't name an alternate, the court will do it for you unless you explicitly state in the trust document that no one can serve but the trustee you named. In that event, when your trustee can no longer serve, the trust will be dissolved and the property will go to your heirs.

If you name two or more cotrustees, all of them must agree (some states require only a majority) before any investments or distributions can be made. Some grantors who want a group of trustees to serve will give one of the group an overriding veto to avoid standoffs in decision making.

Living trusts usually name the grantor as trustee, or the grantor and grantor's spouse. This allows them to maintain total control over their assets.

Testamentary trusts usually name as trustee the same person chosen as executor of the will. This should be someone who is both likely to survive you and willing to carry out your wishes. Generally, it's best to choose a trusted relative, friend or business associate. If you don't have a friend or relative able and willing to serve, you can appoint a trust company, bank or lawyer, but even then it's best to name a friend or relative to serve as a cotrustee. No financial institution or lawyer knows or cares about your wishes or the need to preserve your property's value as much as a trusted friend or relative would.

Most trust companies tend to invest the funds entrusted to them conservatively. They need to uphold their reputation as careful trust managers and are keenly aware of their legal liabilities. If a beneficiary proves that the firm mishandled trust funds, the company's insurer may have to pay a great deal in damages. This would undermine the trust company's reputation and increase its insurance costs. For these reasons, expect caution, not aggressive investment strategies, if you turn to a trust company for financial management. Trust companies usually charge either a percentage or a fixed fee for their services (see Chapter 8).

THE TRUSTEE'S RESPONSIBILITIES

When you create a trust, you must prepare instructions for the trustee and give the trustee the authority needed to carry them out. You might, for example, restrict the trustee's options by ruling out selling the family home, or you might give the trustee a liberal hand in deciding to which of your children to give money and when.

A court will find several trustee powers implied simply by your creation of a trust, even if those powers aren't stated. If you give no instructions at all, chances are the court will decide that the trustee has broad discretionary powers.

Implied powers include those needed to administer a trust properly, such as the authority to invest the assets and collect the income, which includes opening bank accounts, hiring an accountant, collecting rent, and so on.

You may grant specific powers to all of your trustees, including alternates, or only to the original trustee or cotrustees.

Powers commonly given to trustees include the right to:

- Sell trust property
- Invest proceeds from the sale of property
- Collect the income of trust property
- Use that income to pay taxes or other debts
- Amend the terms of the trust
- Distribute trust funds to beneficiaries

Depending on what power you give your trustee, what you put into the trust is likely to change from time to time during the life of the trust. For example, your trustee may decide to sell a piece of trust property, then deposit the money in a bank account, then use it to buy bonds. Your trust property will have been converted from a house to cash to a bank account to bonds.

If you give your trustee the power to make such investments, you should also include specific instructions about what trust property can or cannot be invested. If you do not leave such instructions, your trustee is free to act on his or her own, although he or she is supposed to exercise care, diligence, skill and prudence when investing trust assets.

THE TRUSTEE'S DUTIES

By law, trustees are required to do several things. If they don't, they may be sued for breach of duty. If you, or your heirs, win such a suit against a trustee, the trustee may be replaced and any losses can be recovered. Trustees must:

- *Take possession of the trust property* as soon as possible after becoming a trustee. This includes all tangible assets (cash, personal property, real estate, etc.) and documents representing intangible assets (partnership agreements, stocks, bonds, bank accounts, certificates of deposit, etc.). Taking control of the assets may either mean simply knowing where they are or actually taking possession of them. For example, a trustee usually must take possession of tangible items like jewelry or cash and put them in a safe place. Some tangible items, however, such as a home's furnishings, stay where they are unless the trust directs otherwise. Ownership documents, such as title to a house, must be collected by the trustee and put into a safe place.
- *Know their duties and instructions,* identify beneficiaries and notify them about the trust and its provisions. This

means that a trustee must read and understand the trust document in order to act on it.

- *Protect and preserve trust property* against challenges that the trust is invalid—unless, of course, it is invalid.
- *Be accountable to beneficiaries.* Typically this involves keeping good records of all transactions involving trust assets, including sales, investments, transfers between accounts and the like.
- *Keep the trust property separate* from the trustee's own property and clearly identify trust property. For example, a trust bank account should have the trustee's name on the account. A trustee may *never* borrow, sell or lease trust assets for his or her personal use.
- *Make sure trust property is productive* by investing it to produce income, as, for example, in an interest-earning account.
- *Pay the beneficiary* as instructed by the trust document or at reasonable intervals.

CAN A TRUSTEE BE REMOVED?

Any party to a trust—a grantor, a trustee or a beneficiary—may petition a court to remove a trustee who is not obeying the trust's directions, who is stealing trust property or who cannot handle the assigned and implied duties.

If you want your beneficiaries or cotrustees to have authority to remove a trustee, you can save everyone time, money and hassle by including what's called a *removal clause:*

> The beneficiaries and cotrustees have the absolute right to fire a trustee at any time and for any cause.

Be aware, however, that such sweeping authority can be abused and that in effect it can turn your trustee into a servant of your beneficiaries or other trustees, not of *your* intentions for the trust. One option is to limit the conditions under which a trustee may be removed by other parties: You may, for example, require that two or more of them agree on the removal, or that a doctor of your choosing must agree that the trustee has become physically or mentally incompetent.

If you do not include a removal clause, however, courts will assume you did not want the trustee removed and will be reluctant to do so unless the beneficiaries can prove that the trustee's behavior is hazardous to the trust and impairs decision making. When no removal clause was written into the trust, courts have removed trustees for habitual drunkenness, dishonesty or a tendency toward personal insolvency. Courts may also remove trustees guilty of violating *(breaching)* a trust by:

* Not obeying trust instructions
* Mingling trust funds with personal funds
* Repeated failure to report the trust's financial condition
* Failure to cooperate with other trustees

The breach must be considered serious and willful, however. A court usually will not remove a trustee who simply made an honest mistake, or who acted in good faith, unless the good-faith actions resulted in a big loss for the trust.

If a trustee is removed, the alternate trustee steps in. If you did not name one, the court usually listens to the beneficiaries' recommendations when appointing a successor.

CAN A TRUSTEE QUIT?

You should also include in your trust instructions for how a trustee can resign. If you've left no instructions, a trustee who wants to resign must get court approval; it will not be enough simply to notify the beneficiaries. This situation might arise, for example, if a trustee finds that the duties are taking too much time or require skills or abilities he or she doesn't have. If a trustee's resignation will endanger or inconvenience the beneficiaries (for instance, if the trustee is, at that time, transacting trust business, such as closing the sale of a house), a court will not allow the resignation, at least not until a reasonable amount of time has passed to remove the risk or inconvenience to the trust's assets and beneficiaries.

HOW IS A TRUSTEE PAID?

A trustee is legally entitled to be compensated for services. Serving as a trustee, after all, can require considerable skill, time and effort and brings with it a risk of being sued by the beneficiaries for not doing the job right.

If you do not want your trust to incur the expense of paying your trustees, you can appoint yourself (in the case of a living trust) or someone whom you know will not charge for the service. If you select a bank or other institution as trustee, expect to have to pay them; the amount they may charge is set by law and is typically a percentage of the trust funds they manage. If more than one trustee serves, each trustee may collect the statutorial amount allowed.

If a trustee's fee is challenged in court, the court will have to decide if it's reasonable. Usually, such a determination is based on the difficulty of the work, the value and nature of the trust property, and the results of the trustee's work.

SELECTING A BENEFICIARY

This should be easy: You probably already had beneficiaries in mind when you first considered drafting a trust. You may name any person or corporation as your beneficiary. You may name specific individuals (for example, "Deborah and David Plante") or a class of individuals ("the children of

Deborah and David Plante"). All beneficiaries are presumed to have equal shares in the trust property unless the trust document directs otherwise.

Typical beneficiaries include:

* A spouse, children or grandchildren
* Specific relatives, friends, neighbors, coworkers or employees
* A mentally or physically disabled dependent
* A financially irresponsible person *(spendthrift)*
* A family business
* A charitable organization
* Unborn children; for example, "all children born to my daughter"

In most states, you cannot name as your trust beneficiary a pet or inanimate object because the law doesn't consider either of these a person. A person or corporation can sue in court; your dog or car cannot. If you want to make sure your collie or antique Mercedes-Benz is cared for after you die, give the dog or car to a friend with care instructions and put money for the dog or car's care into a trust, with the friend as trustee and beneficiary.

You do not need to use special or legal language to name a beneficiary in a trust document, but you do have to be clear enough that all parties know whom you mean, including a court if a dispute should arise. Ambiguous language could create confusion. No one will know who "my best friend" is unless you identify the friend by full legal name and, to be safe, some other identifier, such as an address or Social Security number.

In general, the person to whom you want to leave property should be identified by name and relationship to you. For example, "I leave my 1989 Toyota Celica to my friend Linda Byrne." In the unlikely event that you have more than one friend named Linda Byrne, you should put her address down as well.

You should also name alternate *(contingent)* beneficiaries in case your first *(primary)* beneficiaries die or decline to accept the trust assets. By naming alternate beneficiaries, you continue to maintain control over who will get your property and ensure the continuity of your trust even if the primary beneficiaries die.

If you don't name an alternate, any number of things could happen: The trustee might appoint a new beneficiary; the trust property might go to the heirs of the primary beneficiaries, whether or not that's what you wanted; the property could revert back to you; or, when you die, the property could go to your estate and have to be probated. The only way you can exercise control over such matters is by naming alternate beneficiaries in the trust document.

Finally, you should select *residual* beneficiaries. When a trust is dissolved, these persons inherit whatever is left in the trust that has not been designated for other beneficiaries.

CAN A MINOR BE A BENEFICIARY?

Minors are often selected as trust beneficiaries, but there may be limits on how much money or property they are allowed to receive. Some states do not allow minors to receive outright gifts of more than a relatively low amount—$5,000, for example. To get around these limits, the money or property may be passed to the minor through a legal guardian, custodian or trustee.

Most states have a law (either the Uniform Gift to Minors Act or Uniform Transfers to Minors Act) that allows adults to transfer any amount of cash, real estate, business interest and the like to minors free of probate. The property must be irrevocably transferred and must be managed for the benefit of the minor by a custodian until the minor reaches the age of majority, at which time the property must be handed over.

CHAPTER 7

FUNDING
THE TRUST

What properties do most people put into a trust? Do they fund the trust with their home? short-term investments? bank accounts? stocks and bonds? How should the property be described in your trust document? What do you have to do to transfer property into a trust? This chapter answers questions such as these.

WHAT SHOULD YOU INVEST?

You may fund a trust with anything you own. You may put into it cash, stocks, bonds, a bank or money market account, a mutual fund account, personal property, real estate, your home, your life insurance policy, your future retirement benefits; in short, any item you own or have the right to transfer can be put into a trust.

What you decide to put into a trust is a different matter. It depends on what you want the trust to do. If your sole purpose is to bypass probate, then it's in your interest to put into a revocable living trust everything you own, or at least big-ticket items not already destined to bypass probate through joint tenancy or other means. One popular item included in revocable living trusts is the family home, but you may also include a personal bank account, insurance proceeds or even cash.

If you're setting up a trust for your child's education, on

the other hand, you probably want to include only the money needed to pay educational costs and trustee fees. If you also want the child to receive his or her entire inheritance upon college graduation, you would also include whatever you want the child to inherit.

WHAT DO YOU OWN?

Before deciding what to put into your trust, you should know what you own. This might seem a simple task at first, but there are a few twists. Ask yourself, for example, who owns the family home that your wife's family gave her 30 years ago and in which you've since invested well over $250,000. Until you know the answers to such questions, you can't create your trust using the house.

So, who does own it? That depends on the ownership papers. When you buy property with someone else, whether that is your spouse or not, you must use one of three types of ownership agreements: *tenancy in common, joint tenancy with right of survivorship* or *tenancy by the entirety.* These ownership arrangements can apply to real estate or to business or personal property.

If you're married and live in one of the nine community property states, what you own is governed also by community property laws. And, in states that don't have such laws, you must be aware of special statutes that prevent you from disinheriting your spouse.

Tenancy in Common

If your ownership agreement is unclear as to who owns your property and how, state laws give preference to tenancy in common. This legal phrase simply means you own the percentage of the property you paid for. If you bought a house with two other people and each contributed the same amount, you each own a third unless you specified differently in your agreement.

You can do what you want with your one third of the property, as can the co-owners (called *tenants*). You can sell your share, put it into a trust, leave it to someone in your will, even give it away—all without permission from your co-owners. If you die, your third goes to probate as part of your estate, unless you've put it into a trust. Many ownership agreements specify tenancy in common.

Joint Tenancy with Right of Survivorship

Joint tenancy differs from tenancy in common in two key ways: it allows you to create a survivorship arrangement, and your co-owners must consent to anything done with the property.

The survivorship arrangement should be written explicitly into your ownership agreement. It means that when you die, the property goes directly to your co-owner, without stopping for probate. If you have such a survivorship arrangement, a court will not allow you to leave your part of the property to someone else, either in your will or in a testamentary trust. And if you want to put such property into a living trust or do anything else with it, you may or may not need the permission of your co-owners, depending on the law in your state.

Tenancy by the Entirety

Tenancy by the entirety is almost identical to a joint tenancy with right of survivorship. The only distinction is that the co-owners must be a married couple and neither spouse has the right to sell or give away the property or place it into a trust without the other's consent. While both spouses are living, the terms of ownership can be altered only by divorce or mutual agreement.

About half the states still recognize tenancy by the entirety. Some even assume that all property acquired during marriage is owned in tenancy by the entirety unless clearly specified otherwise in the ownership papers.

Community Property

Nine states (Arizona, California, Idaho, Louisiana, Nevada, New Mexico, Texas, Washington and Wisconsin) have community property ownership laws. These apply only to married couples. In these states, each spouse automatically owns half of all the couple's property. The only exceptions are items acquired before marriage and gifts or inheritances specifically given to only one spouse. Thus, in a community property state, it doesn't matter whose name is on the deed to the ranch, who brings home the paycheck or who buys the car: If the purchase is made or the money is earned while the couple is married, it is community property and half of it belongs to each of them.

Your half of the community property ordinarily must go through probate and is part of your taxable estate, even if you leave it to your spouse. This practice varies from state to state, however: California, for instance, has abolished probate for property that passes directly from spouse to spouse, and some states give a surviving spouse a choice as to whether to probate community property.

If you are creating a trust in a community property state, you may put into it only half of what you and your spouse own—unless, of course, your spouse creates the trust with you and contributes the other half.

Common-law States

In states that do not have community property laws, common law applies: The spouse whose name is on the title to a piece of property (a home, a checking account, a stock certificate) is considered the owner. If ownership is unclear, the court will decide who owns it by considering how much each person paid, cared for or used the asset. You should be sure about an asset's ownership before you put it into a trust.

Common-law states give the surviving spouse a legal right to a certain portion of the other spouse's estate—usually a third to a half. Under the Uniform Probate Code (see Appendix I for states that have adopted this code), the spouse's share increases with the length of the marriage, so that the spouse's portion is half of the couple's combined assets after the couple is married for 15 years. However the portion is calculated, the right is called the *spouse's minimum share*. No matter what your will or trust says, your surviving spouse has a right to the legal percentage of your estate. In a few states the exact amount will depend on whether you have children and, in most common-law states, whether the spouse will also inherit property outside of a will—from a trust, for example.

Quasi–Community Property

When a married couple moves into a community property state and brings assets acquired in a common-law state while the spouses were married to each other, those assets are called quasi–community property. When one spouse dies, the assets are treated as community property and the surviving spouse owns only half. However, for federal estate tax purposes, quasi–community property is taxed as separate property, not as community property. This is a concern only to couples whose combined estates are worth more than $600,000.

In these situations, you can put into a trust only half of your quasi–community property—again, unless your spouse joins you in creating the trust and contributes the other half.

HOW SHOULD THE PROPERTY BE DESCRIBED?

The property you put into your trust can be listed and described on a form called a *trust schedule;* if you're creating a testamentary trust, you need to list its assets in your will. Some professionals may advise against describing your assets on a trust schedule because they think it's a waste of time as long as those assets have been retitled into the name of your trust. Other professionals strongly encourage listing your assets, not so much for your benefit but for the benefit of your trustee and beneficiaries, who won't have to spend time tracking down your assets.

While it's important to be specific in describing the assets, don't go overboard. You certainly don't need a lot of legalese or lengthy descriptions. For example, if you want to put your house into a trust, identify it by its street address: "The house and real estate located at 5142 MacArthur Blvd., Small Town, VA 22202." You do not need to include lot numbers, county names or other legal descriptions, but if not including legal descriptions on important assets like real estate makes you nervous, go ahead and do it. You'll find the legal description (lot number and all) on the deed or title.

Household furnishings can be listed generally as well: ". . . and all personal property and household furnishings located at 5142 MacArthur Blvd., Small Town, VA 22202."

If you want to put cash into your trust, do not simply list the dollar amount. You need to state where the money is to come from—for example: "My savings account No. 435-310-2, Thrifty Savings, Midland, MI, with a current balance of about $10,000."

If you're setting up a testamentary trust, however, it's better not to name the bank, because over the years, you're likely to change banks. Instead, in your trust state, "$10,000 of my cash assets is to become part of the principal of my testamentary trust."

HOW TO TRANSFER PROPERTY TO A TRUST

Transferring property to a trust is called *funding* the trust. You fund testamentary and living trusts differently.

As noted, because a testamentary trust is created in your will, property placed in it must first go through probate. In effect, your testamentary trust remains empty, or unfunded, until you die. After your property goes through probate, the trustee identified in your will must change the titles to the property into the trust's name.

If you are creating a *revocable* living trust, you can either fund it immediately or leave it unfunded until a certain time or event occurs. An *irrevocable* living trust is always funded; otherwise, there would be no reason to set one up (see Chapter 10).

Bear in mind that if you leave a living trust unfunded, you run the risk that your property will not escape probate when you die. It may not even go to the beneficiaries you designated in the trust. That's because the property will still be in your name and considered yours, not the trust's. It is your responsibility, unless you assign it to someone else, to transfer your property's ownership to the trust. You do this by changing the ownership papers on each item placed into the trust.

Some grantors transfer property by putting it in the trustee's name. Others put it in the name of the trust itself. If you're both grantor and trustee, you can do it either way, but if you're not the trustee, we recommend you transfer ownership to the person you name to manage the trust. For example, you would transfer assets to "Beverly Burck, Trustee of the Michael T. Kelly Revocable Living Trust."

Transferring loose items—things for which you have no ownership papers—is done by making a general statement about those items on your trust schedule: "All my personal property and household furnishings."

To transfer property for which you do have ownership papers—vehicles, bank accounts, real estate, stocks, bonds, insurance policies, and so on—you need to reregister the property in question in the name of the trust. For example, title to an insurance policy in the name of Deborah R. Atkins would become a title in the name of "The Deborah R. Atkins Revocable Living Trust." However, if Deborah is not the trustee of her own trust, the new title should read, for example, "Lynne Lester, trustee of The Deborah R. Atkins Revocable Living Trust." In many instances, a broker or agent will complete the necessary paperwork for a small fee.

Transferring a house to a trust is typically done by the trustee or by the trustee's lawyer. If Deborah wants to do it herself, she would need to complete, sign and have notarized a correction deed (in some states called a quitclaim, grant or trust transfer deed) to transfer her house to her revocable living trust. After locating her original deed, she would purchase a correction deed form from a local legal stationery store, complete it, sign it in front of a notary and take it to the Recorder of Deeds in the county where her real estate is located.

In most states, transferring real estate to a revocable living trust should not affect property taxes in any way. To be on the safe side, you should call the Recorder of Deeds to see whether there are any transfer taxes involved or whether transferring property to a trust will trigger a reassessment of your property taxes. Chances are it won't.

If you own property with someone else, whether your spouse or not, you may need to get approval from the other owner or owners before you change the ownership papers. Many states even require that your spouse sign a consent form before you're allowed to transfer property you own together, especially real estate. Check the form of your ownership and the rules governing it and get any approvals you need in writing. Of course, most institutions—banks, lenders, insurance companies, and so on—will want your co-owners' signed agreement before allowing the name change. Be prepared to meet these requirements.

CHAPTER 8

GETTING HELP

A variety of trust services is available—for a price. Estate-planning specialists and nonspecialists include high-priced estate and tax lawyers, certified public accountants (CPAs), insurance agents, financial planners and lower-cost legal clinics, legal services plans and paralegals. This chapter discusses the various options and suggests when to consider hiring help and when using do-it-yourself materials should suffice.

At the outset, it's worth noting that you should hire a professional to draft or at least review your trust if your estate is worth more than $600,000 and your primary purpose is to avoid taxes, if you are creating a charitable trust or if you need to address complicated family or personal circumstances, such as providing for a child who is receiving government benefits. However, if your needs are simple and you know you want to prepare a revocable living trust, you can either take advantage of the low-cost alternatives discussed below or draft the trust yourself.

LOW-COST OPTIONS

Before deciding how to prepare your trust, you should explore your alternatives, including the following economical sources of legal service:

Legal Clinics

You can get help from a legal clinic on most legal matters, including drafting a trust, for somewhat less than the going rate among local law firms. A Hyatt Legal Services clinic in Washington, D.C., for example, quotes $995 as a "ballpark" figure for drafting a living trust. (That price, which is typical among legal-clinic chains, does not, however, include transferring property to the trust.) If your needs are simple, a legal clinic is definitely worth looking into, but shop around and compare services and prices before buying: As with regular law firms, the quality of service you get and the cost of that service will vary from clinic to clinic.

Legal clinics can offer services at competitive rates because they limit themselves to routine cases, streamline operations with standard forms and hire newly trained lawyers and paralegals.

Legal Services Plans

Legal services plans operate like health maintenance organizations (HMOs) in that they stress preventive care and serve a defined group of clients. The plans started as an employer-paid benefit for union members but have since become widely available to other groups and even to private individuals. According to the National Resource Center for Consumers of Legal Services, more than 58.3 million Americans were estimated to be enrolled in such plans as of August 1990.

Some plans require a membership fee up front; these are often called "prepaid" plans. Others simply charge enrolled members reduced rates for services rendered. If you belong to a group plan, chances are your employer or union picks up all or most of the membership fee. If you belong to a private or individual plan, you probably pay an annual membership fee of about $100.

Many group plans offer comprehensive services, including drafting trusts, often as part of your will. Private plans, like those offered by Montgomery Ward or Prepaid Legal Services, Inc., offer more limited benefits. Although your membership in such a private plan may include unlimited legal advice over the telephone, plus will preparation and legal review of documents up to six pages long, chances are you'll have to pay extra to have a trust drafted. How much extra you will be charged depends on the plan and the complexity of your trust, but most plan lawyers will probably charge 25 to 35 percent less than the going rate among local lawyers. If you're already a plan member, it's worth asking about the cost of drafting a trust, but if you aren't, the savings probably won't be enough to make joining a plan worthwhile if a simple trust is all you expect to buy. On the other hand, if it's a complete family estate planning service you're shopping for, the savings may well be more than the cost of joining a plan.

Independent Paralegals

Independent paralegals offer routine legal services to the public. Paralegals do not have a law degree or a license to practice law, but many of them have experience working in law firms and some have attended paralegal school. Independent paralegals typically offer one or, at most, two specialized services and can develop a high level of competence in those services simply by repeatedly preparing the same forms. Independent paralegals charge from a third to a half of what local lawyers charge.

Be aware, however, that independent paralegals are not allowed to provide legal advice: They may not tell you what kind of trust is best for you, may not advise you how to complete a trust form and may not explain trust laws to you.

The best way to find an independent paralegal is by word of mouth or by searching newspaper or Yellow Pages advertisements. In the Yellow Pages, look under "Paralegals" or "Typing services."

DOING IT YOURSELF

The high demand for materials to help people prepare their own trusts is evidenced by the wide variety of do-it-yourself kits, books, legal forms and computer software now on the market.

Do *not* try to prepare your own trust if you do not have the time or willingness to read up on the subject, to compare different trusts and to devote time and effort to drafting the document. You should also seek professional help and not attempt to set up the trust yourself if your estate is worth $600,000 or more and your primary purpose is to shelter it from taxes, if you want to create a charitable trust or if someone in your family has special needs—for example, if you want to provide for the care of a disabled child.

If your needs are simple, if you only have to provide for yourself or wish to leave everything to your spouse and children, a number of books and kits are available to help you. Not all self-help material will meet your needs, however. Some kits, for instance, may not provide for a married person to leave property to anyone other than his or her spouse. Shop around for a kit or book that does what you want. If you can't find what you're looking for, you probably should ask a professional for help.

When using do-it-yourself materials, always look at the copyright date to make sure you're getting up-to-date information. If the book or kit has been in print more than two or three years, look for something more recent. In any event, you may want to take your draft document to a professional for review. The older the do-it-yourself materials you are using, the more important this becomes.

DO-IT-YOURSELF HELP

Books

Several do-it-yourself publications are on the market, especially for writing revocable living trusts. The best known is Norman Dacey's *How to Avoid Probate!* It includes a wide array of forms for preparing a living trust and advises that you put everything you own—house, bank account, business interests—into a trust to avoid probate. Dacey's approach is to draft a separate living trust for each type of asset, one for the home, another for the family business, another for bank accounts and so on. That may be fine for people who want to put only a single asset into a trust, but for others it could become unwieldy. Other books combine the types of assets you can put into one trust. Which is best for you depends on your needs.

Kits and Software

Many more kits and computer software programs are on the market for writing a will or writing a will with a trust than for writing a trust alone. In fact, few software kits have been developed solely for writing trusts, even simple ones, though there may be more soon. Only a decade ago, it was rare to see a will kit on the market; now they are commonplace. New software is always being developed, especially in response to public demand, so continue checking bookstores and software stores.

For a list of do-it-yourself materials, see Appendix VII.

ESTATE-PLANNING PROFESSIONALS

Lawyers

Many people hire a lawyer to draft a trust. If that's your inclination, bear a few things in mind.

First, a license to practice law is no assurance that the lawyer has ever prepared a trust before, or even that the lawyer has read as much about trusts as you have.

Second, like other professionals, lawyers tend to recommend what they already know how to do. If your lawyer has drafted 20 bypass trusts in the past and has that particular form already in a computer, expect a strong recommendation that you use a bypass trust even if it's not necessarily the best for you.

Third, if your estate is complex and you want "the best," you'll pay for it—both in fees and in the time and effort you will have to devote to shopping. If your requirements are relatively simple, however, you probably don't need an estate-planning specialist, whether it's a lawyer or not.

Ask for recommendations from friends, relatives, neighbors or business associates. Other options are to ask your local or state bar association for the names of estate-planning lawyers and to check your library for directories; however, neither the bar nor the directories will recommend one estate-planning lawyer over another.

After you've found several good prospects, schedule in-person interviews. These initial consultations are usually free or offered at reduced rates. Ask about each lawyer's experience in drafting trusts, especially to meet needs and circumstances similar to yours; how much it will cost you; whether the lawyer will put the fee in writing; and if you can have a list of previous clients for whom each lawyer has prepared trusts.*

Before discussing fees, the lawyer may want to know more about what you want, so come prepared to share information about your personal and financial background. This is best done by preparing an inventory of your assets (Appen-

*For tips on hiring and using lawyers, we suggest *Using a Lawyer . . . And What to Do If Things Go Wrong,* by Kay Ostberg in association with HALT, Random House, 1990.

dix IV has an inventory form you can use) and sharing your thoughts on what type of trust you're interested in.

A good estate-planning lawyer will advise you on the types of trusts that can meet your goals and explain the legal and tax consequences of each. The lawyer will also advise you on how to transfer your property to a trust.

Don't go into a lawyer's office to talk about fees and services before you've finished reading this book. At the very least, the information in it will arm you with questions you should ask about why the lawyer recommends one trust over another. Don't just take his or her word for it. If you don't understand the reasoning, don't buy it. Don't accept "for tax considerations" as a complete answer. Ask what those "considerations" are.

The price of having a lawyer draft your trust depends on the type of trust you want and where you live. Some lawyers charge by the hour (anywhere from $65 to $300 an hour and up), while others charge a flat fee ($500 and up—mostly up).

A simple revocable living trust that requires little or no federal estate tax planning typically will cost just under $1,500 in a lawyer's office, whether you're single or married with children. A lawyer who is a tax and planning specialist may charge more. The price is for gathering background information—both personal and financial—and drafting the trust. It does not include changing title to your property or changing the trust in the future. Prices are slightly lower for testamentary trusts. Try to be sure the cost is for the time and expertise involved, not the value of your assets. It is no more difficult to prepare a trust for $3 million in stocks than one for $1 million in stocks. The work should cost the same.

You can also hire a lawyer to review a trust you've drafted yourself or to make adjustments to an existing trust, such as amending it to take advantage of changes in trust or tax law. Ironically, amending a trust may cost more than having a trust drafted from scratch. To avoid liability problems for a document they didn't originally draft, many lawyers will take extra time to review your work and recheck the trust laws.

Other ways to keep legal fees to a minimum include developing a good idea of what you want ahead of time, supplying the attorney with up-to-date information about your finances, asking if a legal secretary or paralegal can help do some of the work to keep costs down and volunteering to transfer property titles to the trust yourself.

Accountants

Most accountants will not draft a trust for you because they could be brought up on charges of practicing law without a license. However, they will tell you whether they think you need one.

At the least, a personal accountant will be more familiar with your financial situation and need less time to form an expert opinion than any other professional you might contact. If you already use an accountant who is familiar with your financial circumstances, ask whether you should use a trust in your estate plan. Some accountants are well versed in how to avoid estate taxes and are strong proponents of avoiding probate. Yours might have helpful suggestions about your trust and might even review it. Just as with lawyering, however, a license to practice accounting doesn't mean the accountant is an expert on trusts.

If you don't already have an accountant, you probably won't want to hire one just for this advice. But if you do have one, by all means get his or her opinion.

Trust Officers

Trust officers work for banks. They are hired to manage and invest property that has been put into a trust. If you use a bank as your trustee, one of its trust officers will actually perform the services of trustee. For that reason, trust officers are more often appointed in testamentary trusts than in living trusts, where grantors more often serve as their own trustees.

Trust officers will tell you what kinds of investments they are likely to make if given discretion, how often accounting will be made and how much money their services will cost. Some may be able to draft the trust for you or to suggest language or specific provisions you should include. At the least, they can suggest lawyers to prepare the document for you. Their suggestions are only that—suggestions. No bank can require that you use any law firm or attorney. You can select whomever you want.

Usually, trustee fees are assessed annually and are based on the value of the trust property. Fees are generally 1 percent or less, with a minimum of $750 to $1,000 a year. Other fees may be charged as well, and you should find out about them. For example, ask about fees for preparing tax forms, for withdrawing property from the trust and for terminating the trust. Because of all these fees, unless your trust property is worth at least $100,000, it makes little economic sense to hire a bank as trustee.

Insurance Agents

If you're thinking of setting up an insurance trust (see Chapter 15), you may want to consult an insurance agent about transferring your insurance policy. The agent will probably type up a new policy naming your trust as the owner or beneficiary. If you do not already have life insurance, an agent can explain what types are available and which are best suited for a trust. An agent can also help get your policy into the trust by providing the insurance company's forms to assign ownership to your trust. A Chartered Life Underwriter (CLU) can be particularly helpful with this. Check with a few agents before you make a decision. Compare the policies they recommend, the costs and benefits. In recent years there have been some major insurance company failures. Try to find out about the financial health of the company that is being recommended.

Financial Planners

Financial planners have business and investment backgrounds. Typically, they studied to become Masters in Business Administration (MBAs) or Certified Financial Planners (CFAs). For an hourly fee of up to $125, they will examine your "financial picture" and render an opinion as to how to invest your money, pay your taxes and plan your retirement and estate. Although financial planners do not draft trusts, they will let you know if you can benefit from one, explain the types available and suggest professionals who can draft what you need. They can also help any professional you choose by passing along your financial information. You should choose a financial planner very carefully: Check with other clients, check their education and experience and also get a good idea of the planner's track record and honesty. If you already have a financial planner, by all means consult him or her. It probably does not make sense, however, to hire one only to consult about trusts.

PART III

LIVING AND TESTAMENTARY TRUSTS

CHAPTER 9

REVOCABLE LIVING TRUSTS

This chapter discusses revocable living trusts, the most popular trusts for estates worth $600,000 or less. A revocable living trust is a legal instrument that you establish while you are still alive to manage some or all of your assets and that you retain the power to amend or cancel at any time.

In this chapter, you'll learn why such trusts are so popular—their advantages, disadvantages and tax considerations. You'll also find sample language you can use in drafting a simple living trust for estates valued at less than $600,000.

WHO NEEDS A LIVING TRUST?

You don't have to own a giant corporation or have enormous wealth to enjoy the benefits of a revocable living trust. In recent years, these trusts have become popular with middle-income individuals and married couples who have discovered that the device can provide them with income during their lives and save their assets from the expense and delays of probate when they die.

Although typically used by individuals and married couples, nonmarried couples can also create living trusts with property they own jointly.

In most cases, people create living trusts so they can pass their assets quickly and efficiently to their beneficiaries without having those assets eroded by lawyers' and other fees. Because the major goal of these trusts is avoiding probate, they typically end shortly after the grantor dies and the assets are distributed.

EXAMPLE

Louise and Frank, who are in their 60s, own a $120,000 house, $45,000 in stocks and $25,000 in bank certificates of deposit. They put all their major assets—home, stocks and savings— into a revocable living trust and live on the income produced by those assets. When they die, the assets go directly to their daughter, Barbara, without passing through probate. Barbara will get it all; none will have to be sold off to pay lawyers or probate fees.

EXAMPLE

John, a 70-year-old bachelor, owns an $80,000 condominium, $50,000 in other real estate, a $50,000 life insurance policy and personal items worth about $50,000. He sets up a revocable living trust so that when he dies, his assets will go to his nephews, Robert and Kevin, without going through probate.

Louise, Frank and John haven't tied up their assets forever. Revocable living trusts can be canceled or changed any time. If they need to take large amounts of cash out of the trust, say for a medical emergency or a vacation, they can do it immediately, without penalty. Louise and Frank might cash in their CDs, while John might borrow from his life insurance.

REVOCABLE LIVING TRUSTS AND TAXES

As noted in Chapter 5, revocable living trusts *do not offer any tax advantages.* However, you can transfer the following property, in or outside of a trust, without incurring federal estate taxes:

- Any assets totaling less than $600,000 to whomever you want (providing you haven't used up your $600,000 exemption by giving away more than $10,000 a year to anyone; see Chapter 5)
- All assets that you pass on to your spouse when you die
- All assets you leave to charity

If a couple's combined assets are worth more than $600,000, a surviving spouse's estate will be taxed on any amount above $600,000. To avoid this, many couples set up a bypass and QTIP trust (see Chapter 13), which allows them, in effect, to double the federal estate tax exemption, passing up to $1.2 million to their heirs without paying federal estate tax.

Advantages

Revocable living trusts have a number of benefits:

Probate: You completely avoid the expense and delays of probate.

Revocability: You may change or cancel the trust anytime you want. If you don't like how the trust is working, you may change it.

Asset management: You control how the assets are managed, or, if you prefer, you can let another person or a corporation manage the assets for you. And your assets continue to be managed by someone you trust if you become unable to manage them yourself.

Asset inventory: A living trust helps you put your financial house in order by encouraging you to account for all of your possessions and gather together all of your legal documents.

Court challenges: A living trust is less likely to be challenged in court than a will is.

Income: You may continue to receive income from your assets or let it accumulate in the trust.

Spendthrift protection: You may include a provision that protects the trust's assets from the creditors of your beneficiaries (but not your own creditors).

Avoid Probate   Avoiding probate may be the biggest advantage of revocable living trusts. It certainly is a consideration uppermost in the minds of most people who decide to create one.

As illustrated in Chapter 2, probate can eat up a large chunk of your estate when you die, but assets placed in a revocable living trust don't have to go through probate at all. This can save your beneficiaries thousands of dollars.

A living trust provides for the quick, efficient distribution of your assets without lawyers or courts. All your appointed trustee needs is a copy of your death certificate to begin distributing or managing your assets as instructed in your trust. If, instead of putting your assets into a trust, you were to write them into your will, your executor might be forced to wait up to a year or more before distributing them to your heirs.

Change or Cancel It Anytime   Another important feature of the living trust is that it may be changed *(amended)* or canceled *(revoked)* anytime and for any reason. You might want to change or cancel it if you or your spouse becomes seriously ill, if you divorce or remarry, if a beneficiary dies, if you sell your home or other asset you had placed into it or if you move to another state. In some states, any provision for your spouse is automatically revoked if you and your spouse get divorced.

You change the document by executing, signing and dating an amendment form (see page 93) and delivering it to your trustee. If you prefer, you can hire legal help to make the changes.

Special caution for married couples: A married couple's living trust may be altered only while both spouses are alive, and both must agree to the change. If one spouse dies, the trust becomes irrevocable and the surviving spouse is not allowed to make any changes in it.

Most living trusts for couples operate this way so each spouse can be assured that the assets will be distributed after his or her death according to the original plans. For example, a surviving husband who remarries would not be allowed to make his new wife the trust's beneficiary, nor could he decide to delete as trust beneficiaries his children from his marriage to his first wife.

(You can circumvent this limitation, however, by including specific language that gives the surviving spouse what's called a *power of appointment.* This gives the survivor authority to make changes in the trust. Such provisions are discussed in more detail in Chapter 13.)

Spouses may also set up their trust so that when one of them dies, some of the assets of that spouse are given immediately to the designated beneficiaries. For example, a mother might direct that the trust pass her jewelry on to her daughter; when he dies, a father might pass on his car to his son or other beneficiary, whether or not his wife survives him. However, the bulk of a married couple's assets could and usually does remain in the trust to benefit the surviving spouse until that spouse also dies.

If the spouses name themselves as trustees, the surviving spouse becomes the sole trustee and he or she continues to control the trust and to receive income from it. When the surviving spouse dies, the remaining assets are distributed to the beneficiaries. (For more information about trusts set up by married couples, see Chapter 13.)

Maintain Control of its Management A living trust allows you to maintain complete control over and to manage your assets while you're alive. You, not the courts, name the beneficiaries, appoint guardians for minors or disabled relatives and select backup *(successor)* trustees.

You also decide how and when your assets are to be invested. If you'd rather leave that decision to someone you think can handle your financial affairs better, you can appoint someone else as trustee. Of course, you should expect to pay for this service.

Appointing someone else as trustee while you're still alive gives you another benefit: You get to see how your property probably will be managed by your trustee after you're gone and how your beneficiaries will react. If you learn that adjustments or further instructions are needed, you can simply amend your trust.

Properly drawn up, your living trust also guards you and your family from losing control of your assets if you can't manage them because of illness, injury or other reasons. That's because you, not the courts, decide in the trust whom you want to manage your assets if you can't.

Court Challenge   Living trusts are not likely to be challenged in court because they, unlike wills, are private documents that ensure your privacy. You don't have to notify any of the people named in the trust—or those who are not named in the trust. Nor do death notices have to be placed in local newspapers when you die, as they do with a will—a process that can bring forward family members and friends looking for distributions you didn't want them to have and to which they aren't entitled.

Income   You may set up your living trust to provide you and your spouse with income as long as you live. As trustee, you will still manage and invest your assets as necessary, but you may have the trust pay you a certain percentage of its value or its annual income at intervals you choose. (When it comes time to pay taxes, you report any income received from your trust on your regular income tax forms—a separate tax form for the trust is still required, but on it you merely indicate the amount of trust income and say that it is reported on your regular income tax forms.)

Spendthrift Provision If you set up a living trust to support your children after you die but are worried about their foolish spending habits, you may restrict access to the trust's funds. A spendthrift clause, such as the one found on page 90, prohibits the beneficiaries from giving or selling to others their rights to the trust's assets or income. That means the trust's assets are also protected from the beneficiary's creditors.

Cost A trust is more expensive to set up than a will, but once a trust has been created and funded, it takes little money to maintain it, providing the trustee serves without charge.

Disadvantages

Despite the advantages, a revocable living trust also has a number of drawbacks:

Income taxes: It provides no income tax advantages during your lifetime.

Estate taxes: It can't protect you from federal estate taxes on amounts over $600,000 unless you're married and create a trust that gives you a higher federal estate tax exemption.

Complexity: It's more difficult and expensive to create than a simple will.

Creditors' claims: It doesn't stop your creditors from making claims against your assets, even after your beneficiaries own them.

No Tax Advantages While a revocable living trust avoids probate, it won't shelter your assest from income taxes while you're alive or during the year in which you die. That's because you've retained control of the assets while you were alive and received income from the trust.

A revocable living trust also doesn't shield any assets above the exemptions allowed from federal or state estate taxes.

A revocable living trust does, however, have one tax advantage over an irrevocable trust. If the property increases in value between the time you put the property into the trust and the time you die, taxes on the increased value are, in effect, forgiven if the trust is revocable, but not if the trust is irrevocable.

Difficult and Expensive to Create   If you hire a lawyer to draft your trust, it could cost you 8 to 10 times more than a simple will would, according to lawyers we've sampled. However, the biggest expense and trouble may be transferring assets to the trust—your home, other real estate, a family business, a boat. You can do the work of transferring yourself. You'll have to change your deeds to property, including those being held by lenders, and in some states you'll also have to pay a transfer tax when your new deed is filed. This can range from 1 to 3 percent of your property's value.

Changing the ownership of checking and savings accounts and similar assets can be relatively easy, but some financial institutions can take weeks or months to make the changes, and depending on the work involved, they may charge you a fee.

No Deadlines on Claims   This is one advantage a will has over a trust. Because the probate process imposes a deadline on creditors, after a certain period of time has passed after the will is probated, they no longer can get to its assets. A trust sets no deadlines on how long a creditor can attempt to make claims against you. Most states do have laws that impose such a time limit on collecting debts, but unless your state has such a law, your creditors can sue your trust beneficiaries long after you've died and your trust assets have been distributed.

EXAMPLE OF A LIVING TRUST

To create a revocable living trust, you need:

Assets   These can be anything you own: a house, other real estate, cash, savings, stocks, books, art, and so on. Assets you discard regularly—such as cars or clothes—shouldn't be included in a trust.

Trustees   You or, if you're married, you and your spouse typically serve as trustees of a revocable living trust. However, you might also name your children, other family members, friends or a bank or other institution or corporation.

Beneficiaries   Most often these are your children, grandchildren and other family members. However, friends, charities and caretakers for prized pets or possessions can also be beneficiaries.

Trust Document   Once you decide what assets you want to put into the trust and who the trustees and beneficiaries will be, you can begin creating the document. To be sure the trust is legal, it should be in writing, signed by you, and notarized by a notary public.

A trust doesn't have to be written in legalese to be valid, but it does have to contain several specifics: the name of the trust; the creators *(grantors)* and the trustees; a description of your assets; and the names of your beneficiaries and which assets they will receive.

The trust described below is but one example. It's a revocable living trust for a hypothetical married couple with combined assets of less than $600,000. Married couples with an estate valued at more than $600,000 should turn to Chapter 13 for information on how they can avoid paying federal estate taxes for amounts up to $1.2 million.

You'll find many more examples of living trusts—some in plain language, some in legalese—in other estate-planning guides. Also, some bank trust departments will give you copies of their trust documents.

A REVOCABLE LIVING TRUST

Introductory Clause

This clause names you and your spouse as both the grantors and the trustees. It also states the date and address of your residence.

> This revocable living trust agreement was made on November 25, 1991, by Samuel Zackner and Ruth Zackner of 2121 Pleasant Way, Anytown, NY 10011. Samuel and Ruth Zackner are both the grantors and trustees of the trust.

Trust Name

This states the name of the trust.

> This trust shall be known as The Samuel Zackner and Ruth Zackner Revocable Living Trust.

Rule Against Perpetuities Clause

This ensures that your living trust ends before it violates the rule against perpetuities (see Chapter 4).

> Any trust created herein that has not terminated sooner shall terminate twenty-one (21) years after the death of the last survivor of the class composed of Samuel and Ruth Zackner and their children, grandchildren and any of their more remote descendants who are living when the trust is created for purposes of the rule against perpetuities.

Changing and Canceling the Trust

Since this is a revocable living trust, it may be changed or canceled at any time. In this clause, you must state that you want the trust to be revocable.

Samuel and Ruth Zackner reserve the right to change all or part of The Samuel Zackner and Ruth Zackner Revocable Living Trust at any time during their lives. The change must be made in writing, notarized and attached to the original trust document.

Either Samuel or Ruth Zackner may cancel the trust at any time without the other's permission.

Trust Assets

This identifies the assets of the trust. It is suggested that you list all the assets you want to put into the trust on a separate sheet of paper, called a *schedule,* and attach it to the back of the trust document. This will help your trustee and beneficiaries locate your assets at the appropriate time. The assets on the schedule must be described in specifics (see the example in Appendix V).

Samuel and Ruth Zackner, trustees, transfer ownership of all assets listed on attached Schedule A to The Samuel Zackner and Ruth Zackner Revocable Living Trust. Schedule A lists the combined assets of Samuel and Ruth Zackner, who may add or delete any asset at any time.

Trustees

This clause names not only yourselves as trustees, but also the persons you want to succeed you if you die or are otherwise unable to manage the assets. You must state under what conditions a successor trustee takes over the assigned duties.

Samuel and Ruth Zackner shall be the trustees of The Samuel Zackner and Ruth Zackner Revocable Living Trust. When one spouse dies or is declared unable to handle his or her financial affairs by two medical doctors, the sole trustee shall be the surviving or other spouse.

The appointed successor trustees shall manage the trust under the following conditions:

A. If both trustees die at the same time,

B. When the last surviving spouse dies, or

C. If the surviving spouse is not able to manage his or her financial affairs.

Two medical doctors can declare a spouse unable to handle his or her financial affairs.

Under the conditions listed above, the successor trustee shall be Sally Zackner. If Sally Zackner is dead or unable to manage the trust, the successor trustee shall be William Armstrong.

Successor trustees shall have all the rights and responsibilities of the original trustees of this trust. They shall also have the right to appoint their successors, should they become unable to serve. The trustees shall serve without compensation.

Trust Income

The revocable living trust allows you to receive income from the trust as long as you live. This is spelled out here.

However, at times you may need additional income or need to tap into the original assets *(principal)* of the trust; for example, if one spouse is placed in a nursing home or needs a serious operation. You must detail in this clause exactly why and how much extra you can withdraw from the trust.

Samuel and Ruth Zackner, the grantors/trustees, or the successor trustee, shall distribute the trust's principal and income as follows:

A. Net income from the trust shall be paid to Samuel and Ruth Zackner at least once each quarter during their lives.

B. Following the death of one spouse, net income from the trust shall be paid to the surviving spouse for life.

C. If one spouse becomes unable to handle his or her financial affairs, the other spouse may withdraw at any time some or all of the trust principal to care for the ailing spouse.

D. If both spouses become unable to handle their financial affairs, the successor trustee may withdraw at any time some or all of the principal to care for the ailing spouses.

Trustee Powers, Responsibilities

This clause gives the trustees—whether you, your child, a corporation or any successor trustee—the authority to carry out the provisions of the trust while you're alive and instructions on what to do with the assets when you die. The clause also states specifically that neither you nor your successor trustees will have to post bond or go to court to carry out your responsibilities under this trust. It also spells out the limits of trustees' liability and certain record-keeping requirements the trustees must meet.

The trustees and successor trustees shall have the full power and authority allowed by the State of New York to manage the trust and carry out its provisions. To the extent that any such requirement can legally be waived, no trustee shall be required to give any bond or obtain the order or approval of any court in carrying out any power or discretion given in this trust.

The trustee will keep accurate records of all transactions involving assets placed in this trust and make all such records available for inspection by any beneficiary during normal business hours.

When Samuel Zackner dies, the trustee shall pay his valid debts, last expenses and estate taxes from the residue of the trust.

When Ruth Zackner dies, the trustee shall pay her valid debts, last expenses and estate taxes from the residue of the trust.

When one spouse dies, the trust assets will be used to support the surviving spouse and to make any gifts designated by the first to die.

When both spouses have died, the successor trustee shall distribute the remaining trust assets and net income to the named beneficiaries.

Beneficiaries

This clause names the persons you want to inherit your assets after you die. You should name beneficiaries for each spouse separately so that personal items can be distributed after each spouse dies. This clause also states whether your property will be distributed through a *per stirpes* plan (see Chapter 4) if one of your beneficiaries dies before you do.

A. When Samuel Zackner dies, the named beneficiaries shall receive the following assets:
   Paul Zackner, son of Samuel and Ruth Zackner: A rare stamp collection located in a safe in the home of Samuel and Ruth Zackner, 2121 Pleasant Way, Anytown, NY, and all hunting equipment located at the family vacation home at 901 Sun Valley Road, Anytown, FL.
B. When Ruth Zackner dies, the named beneficiaries shall receive the following assets: Sally Zackner, daughter of Samuel and Ruth Zackner: all books in the home library and all personal jewelry belonging to Ruth Zackner located in the master bedroom at 2121 Pleasant Way, Anytown, NY.
C. When both spouses have died, the successor trustee shall distribute all remaining trust assets and income equally to Sally Zackner, daughter of Samuel and Ruth Zackner, if she is then living, and if not to her descendants per stirpes, and Paul Zackner, son of Samuel and Ruth Zackner, if he is then living, and if not to his descendants per stirpes.

Spendthrift Clause

This protects the assets of the trust from claims by creditors.

No interest of any beneficiary of this trust shall be transferable or assignable or subject to the claims of any beneficiary's creditors.

Severability

This prevents the entire document from being ruled invalid if any part of it is found invalid. It is a standard clause inserted into many legal documents.

Even if any part of this trust agreement or any trust created by it is invalid, illegal or inoperable for any reason, the remaining parts still shall continue in effect under the terms of the trust.

Final Clause

This states that your trust obeys the laws of your state. It also repeats the date the trust was created and contains your signatures. The document will not be valid if you and your spouse don't sign it.

To ensure the validity of the trust, you should sign it in front of a notary public. The document doesn't have to be signed by other witnesses; the notary serves as witness.

This trust agreement was created under and shall be governed by the laws of the State of New York.
Executed: November 25, 1991

Spouse's signature *Samuel Zackner*
Spouse's signature *Ruth Zackner*

On this <u>25th</u> day of <u>November</u> , 1991, before me personally appeared Samuel Zackner and Ruth Zackner, known to me to be the individuals described herein and who duly acknowledged to me that they executed this instrument.

James Barrow

(Notary Seal)   Notary Public

Other Clauses

In addition to the typical clauses listed above, you might consider writing in a number of others, including:

- A clause designating a guardian or conservator (someone to take care of your personal needs should you become incompetent)
- A power of attorney designating whom you want to make financial decisions for you if you become incompetent
- An anatomical gift clause donating your organs to a hospital or scientific research center

Before doing this, however, check to see whether such clauses can be legally added to your living trust. In some states, they can't. Also, most estate-planning professionals prefer to draft separate documents dealing with these sensitive issues, though they will often include them in the price of your living trust.

For example, lawyers typically advise against including a "right-to-die" clause in living trusts. Instead, many will suggest that a separate "health care power of attorney" be drafted to deal with that issue. A health care power of attorney authorizes someone of your choice to decide when or whether to discontinue artificial life support if you become disabled or incompetent. By having a separate document drafted to deal with this issue, you can be assured that your living trust remains private.

CHANGING THE TRUST

A revocable trust may be changed *(amended)* at any time while the grantors are living. In fact, you should review your trust every year and update the trust schedule at least every two years to provide current information for your heirs.

You should also review it with an eye for needed changes whenever a major event (birth, death, marriage or divorce) changes the makeup of your family or a major purchase or sale significantly changes what you own and could be included in your trust (home, boat, rental property, new business, stocks, etc.). If you don't update your trust to reflect these changes, some of your assets could end up in probate court or in the hands of the wrong beneficiaries.

If you're married and both spouses are grantors, both must sign each change to make it valid. This ensures that one spouse isn't trying to take assets from the trust or change beneficiaries without the other's knowledge. Of course, as noted earlier, if one spouse has died, the survivor is no longer able to alter the trust unless a provision granting power of appointment was written into the original trust agreement.

You do not need to draft an amendment for each new asset you want to include. All you need to do is retitle the asset into the name of the trust and list a description of it on your trust schedule. You should document major decisions with amendments, however. For example, if you decide to give $15,000 to charity, you would want to document that decision by drafting an amendment and attaching it to the original trust document. You might use a statement similar to the following:

FIRST AMENDMENT TO THE SAMUEL ZACKNER AND RUTH ZACKNER REVOCABLE LIVING TRUST

This amendment to The Samuel Zackner and Ruth Zackner Revocable Living Trust, dated November 25, 1991, was made on March 2, 1992, by Samuel and Ruth Zackner, grantors/ trustees.

Samuel and Ruth Zackner wish to make a contribution of $15,000 to The United Way immediately upon Samuel Zackner's death. The funds will come from their savings account No. 94350, located at First National Bank of Anytown, Anytown, NY.

Except as amended, Samuel and Ruth Zackner confirm the trust as originally created and signed by them on November 25, 1991, reserving the right to change it again.

Executed: March 2, 1992

Spouse's signature ___*Samuel Zackner*___

Spouse's signature ___*Ruth Zackner*___

On this 2nd day of March , 1992, before me personally appeared Samuel Zackner and Ruth Zackner, known to me to be the individuals described herein and who duly acknowledged to me that they executed this instrument.

James Farrow

(Notary Seal)   Notary Public

CANCELING THE TRUST

A revocable trust may also be canceled *(revoked)* any time during the lifetime of the grantors. It's best to cancel a trust whenever amendments become so extensive they make the original document confusing to read. If you want to change most or all of your trust's provisions, it's best that you cancel the old one and write out a new one rather than prepare an amendment for each change you want.

The trust will not be revoked automatically if you fail to remove an asset you've sold or if you neglect to manage its assets. Instead, your income from the trust might dwindle to a trickle.

A trust you and your spouse have created may be canceled by either of you anytime, simply by adding a clause that states:

Samuel and Ruth Zackner created The Samuel Zackner and Ruth Zackner Revocable Living Trust, on November 25, 1991 and may cancel it at any time while either is alive.

As specified in the trust, Samuel and Ruth Zackner cancel the trust and request that all assets and net income in the trust be returned to Samuel and Ruth Zackner.

Executed: March 15, 1992

Spouse's signature *Samuel Zackner*

Spouse's signature *Ruth Zackner*

On this <u>15th</u> day of <u>March</u> , 1992, before me personally appeared Samuel Zackner and Ruth Zackner, known to me to be the individuals described herein and who duly acknowledged to me that they executed this instrument.

James Farrow

(Notary Seal)   Notary Public

CHAPTER 10

IRREVOCABLE LIVING TRUSTS

When properly drafted, irrevocable living trusts can dramatically reduce your income and estate tax liabilities and, like their revocable counterparts, can keep your assets out of probate.

If you're thinking, "Say no more, this trust is for me!" consider this: To gain the tax advantage, you must give up complete control (or *incidents of ownership,* as lawyers say) over the property you place in trust. Once the property is in the trust, you may not personally benefit from it, nor can you amend, revoke or terminate the trust itself. In other words, to get the maximum tax advantage, you may not be the trustee or beneficiary of the trust assets. In fact, the only way to change an irrevocable trust once it's created is to continue adding assets to it.

Is it worth losing total control of your property to save on taxes? Only you—with the help of a tax specialist—can answer that. For many people, the answer is probably no. But for those who can still live comfortably after giving up part of their estate, an irrevocable trust can be a great way to reduce their tax liability. Even they, however, should be absolutely sure they'll never need to have access to that property again.

TAX RAMIFICATIONS

By placing property into an irrevocable living trust, you reduce your income tax liability because you no longer own, nor do you receive income from, that property. You also reduce or eliminate your estate tax liability because the value of the property you give away is deducted from your gross estate and not considered part of your taxable estate.

Remember, you may give away as much as $600,000 without incurring any federal estate tax. If your taxable estate is valued at more than that, you're best advised to transfer at least enough of your assets to the trust to reduce the worth of your remaining estate below the exemption level and take full advantage of the trust's estate tax avoidance benefit.

As good as all this sounds, remember that the beneficiaries will have to pay income tax on distributions of any income earned by the trust assets. This income is taxed at the beneficiaries' income tax rate.

EXAMPLE

Melanie and Jay, who are in the 33 percent tax bracket, want to reduce their income taxes. They create an irrevocable living trust in 1980 and place $200,000 in stocks and bonds into it. They name Tom as trustee and their three children as beneficiaries. Income from the stocks and bonds is allowed to accumulate in the trust until Melanie and Jay die. Year after year, only the trust pays the income taxes on the accumulating income generated by the stocks and bonds. After Melanie and Jay die, Tom distributes the assets and after-tax income to the three beneficiaries, as instructed.

Obviously, a major goal in setting up an irrevocable living trust is to remove some of your property from your gross estate. Will you have accomplished that goal just by setting up an irrevocable trust and putting property in it? It depends. If you don't draft your irrevocable living trust properly, you could reduce or wipe out its tax advantages. Most important, you may not retain *any* interest in the property. For example, you may not place your house in trust and still live in it. Nor can you put money into an irrevocable trust and set up a system whereby the income eventually gets back to you via the beneficiary.

The following are some provisions you might accidentally include in your irrevocable trust document that would subject *you* to paying taxes on the trust's income.

- It pays money to you, even if only once.
- It supports your family.
- It pays life insurance premiums, legal obligations or other bills.
- Its assets are ultimately paid to you, your spouse or your estate.

FUNDING

Income-producing assets—such as stocks, bonds, certificates of deposit and savings accounts—are the best types of assets to put into an irrevocable trust. Why? Because you shift the income tax burden from yourself to your beneficiary. If you still owned the property, you'd have to pay income taxes on it.

While a house, boat or undeveloped piece of land could be placed into an irrevocable trust to avoid probate delays and fees, it won't save you income taxes because the property is not income, nor does it generate income. Such property is more appropriately put into a revocable trust, where it can avoid probate without the loss of control an irrevocable trust entails (see Chapter 9).

Advantages

Irrevocable living trusts have a number of advantages:

Probate: Assets are not subject to the delays or expense of probate.

Estate tax: Estate taxes are reduced or eliminated because the value of your estate has been reduced by the amount you transfer out of it.

Income tax: The trust reduces your income taxes because you no longer own the assets or the income they generate. However, the trust will have to pay income taxes. And if any income is distributed to a beneficiary, that beneficiary will have to pay taxes on it.

Creditors' claims: Property placed into an irrevocable living trust is immune from your creditors because you no longer own it.

Spendthrift provision: You may include a clause that prohibits beneficiaries from transferring or selling their rights to the trust's assets or income; that protects the trust's assets from the beneficiary's creditors as well.

Disadvantages

Despite the benefits, irrevocable living trusts also carry a number of disadvantages:

Asset use and control: You give up your assets because you may not be either the beneficiary or trustee and still get the tax benefits that are the primary reason for setting up the trust.

Irrevocability: You give up the right to change or cancel the trust.

Income: You may not receive any income from the trust.

Income taxes: You probably can't guarantee that when you die your beneficiaries will be in a lower tax bracket than you were during the lifetime of the trust. If they're in the same or a higher tax bracket when they collect their benefits under the trust, you won't have saved taxes, only postponed them until after your death.

Gift taxes: A federal gift tax return (Form 709) will have to be filed when you turn your assets over to the trust and the value of the trust assets will reduce your $600,000 tax-free allowance at death. State gift taxes may also be involved (for more information on taxes, see Chapter 5).

Complexity: Tax laws governing irrevocable living trusts are fairly complex. Before creating such a trust, consider seeking professional estate-planning advice.

Here's how a typical irrevocable living trust might work:

EXAMPLE

Coralie, a 77-year-old widow, creates an irrevocable living trust to benefit her three grandsons, ages 12, 8 and 6, and names their mother (her daughter) as trustee. She puts $50,000 into the trust and plans to add more each year. The cash is invested in stocks, bonds and bank accounts. She provides that she may never touch the trust assets, even to meet a medical emergency. The trust document instructs her daughter as trustee to let the trust income accumulate until the youngest grandchild reaches age 25 and then to divide the assets equally among the three grandsons. The trust will pay income taxes on the income earned each year. (Of course, if the value of the stocks and bonds declines over the years, they could be left with less than the amount reported for gift tax purposes.)

TYPICAL CLAUSES

An irrevocable living trust contains many of the same clauses the revocable living trust does. For sample language on each provision, refer to Chapter 9. These are the typical provisions to include:

• Naming the trust
• Your name(s) and place of residence

- Names of trustees, successor trustees, beneficiaries and alternate beneficiaries, none of whom can be yourself
- A description of the assets you're placing into the trust
- The names of guardians for minors
- When and how the assets should be distributed
- The powers of the trustee(s)
- Your signature(s) as grantor(s)
- An acknowledgement by and signature of a notary public

Almost all states presume that a trust is irrevocable whether or not the trust explicitly states it. A few states, however, assume that a trust is revocable unless an irrevocability clause is included. To eliminate any confusion, it's always best to include an irrevocability clause. The clause must state clearly that the trust may not be changed or canceled.

> Kathryn Coon, grantor, hereby declares that the Trust Agreement created on July 15, 1990, shall be irrevocable and not subject to modification or amendment.

CHAPTER 11

"POUR-OVER" WILLS

Living trusts are useful, but they can't protect assets that are inadvertently—or intentionally—left outside of the trust's umbrella. That's why many people who have living trusts also include in their estate plan a will that includes a *pour-over* provision.

You can use a pour-over will with either a revocable or irrevocable living trust. Although a pour-over will is not itself a trust, living or otherwise, discussion of it is included here because it complements a living trust in important ways.

The pour-over will typically includes at least these main provisions:

- It identifies you, your spouse and your beneficiaries by name
- It cancels prior wills you've created and amendments to those wills
- It "pours" (transfers) into your trust any assets you've left out of the trust
- It names an executor of the will and gives the executor authority to take the assets through probate. (The executor may or may not be the same person as the trustee of your trust.)

The critical provision is the one that states that if some of your personal or other assets are left out of the trust, they should go into the trust after probate. This guarantees that all of your assets eventually end up in one place and are governed by one distribution scheme—your trust's.

Although it's possible to draft a pour-over will that tries to accomplish a variety of goals—such as transferring assets to your trust, making bequests of personal items outside of your trust and leaving instructions about your burial—it isn't necessary because you can accomplish everything you need with a living trust.

The pour-over will sees to it that after your debts, final expenses and taxes are paid—in other words, after probate—all remaining assets are turned over to the trust, to be distributed with the other trust assets according to the trust's instructions.

Here's sample language for a pour-over will provision that names a trust (through its trustee) as sole heir:

> I give the residue of my estate to Elizabeth Cheever, trustee of The Richard Cheever and Mary Cheever Revocable Living Trust, created August 14, 1991, as amended.

It is important to identify clearly in your pour-over clause which trust is to receive your property, especially if you have more than one trust or if you want to leave property to someone else's trust. That's because you aren't limited to willing your property to a living trust you yourself set up or control, although that's most common. Instead, you can leave it to your sister's trust, your son's, a friend's or anyone else's—even if that person dies before you do. It may even be a trust set up by a business partnership or a charitable institution. All that's required is that the trust that inherits your property be in existence at the time of your death. Under the laws of most states, the trust document must be in existence when you sign your will. To identify in your will the trust your assets will be poured into, state the trust's full legal name, the date it was created and the names of its trustees and beneficiaries.

Advantages

A pour-over will has several advantages:

Revocability: Because it's your will, it may be changed or canceled anytime before you die or become legally incompetent.

Complexity: It's easy to create, and you will not have to spend time and money amending your revocable living trust immediately after you acquire each new asset—a house, rental property or stocks, for example—to include those assets under the instructions in your trust.

Asset management: This is the primary reason for setting up a pour-over will. It anticipates the unpredictable. It also allows you to add to your trust assets of lesser value and those you change often, such as cars, motorcycles and clothing. Any assets left out of the trust or not otherwise mentioned in your will pour into the trust when you die.

This last advantage deserves special comment. Regardless of how careful you are about putting every asset into a living trust, you can't foresee the unforeseeable. For example, should you be killed in a car accident, any settlement money might automatically be transferred to your trust after probate if you included a pour-over clause in your will. If you didn't, your estate would inherit the settlement and the money would be distributed according to your will or, if you died without one, according to the intestacy laws of your state.

EXAMPLE

Pablo and Consuela, a married couple, create a living trust that provides for distribution of the trust assets after both have died. They put all their assets into the trust except two cars, a personal computer, clothing, sports equipment and other personal items. These are left out because they don't want to update their trust with every new acquisition. They also draft a pour-over will that transfers to the estate all assets they left out of their trust. Pablo and Consuela die in a plane crash and their estate eventually receives $1 million from the air car-

rier's insurer. The $1 million, the cars and the personal posses-
sions all pass through probate. Once probate is completed, the
pour-over will kicks in and places all the assets—including
whatever taxes and probate did not extract from the million-
dollar settlement—into the trust, to be distributed to the trust
beneficiaries with the couple's other assets, as outlined in the
trust.

Disadvantages

As you can see from this example, a pour-over will does
have some major drawbacks:

Probate: Any assets left out of the trust and thus included
in the pour-over will must go through probate. This means
delay, trouble and special fees before the beneficiaries can
receive the assets.

Creditors' claims: Assets included in a pour-over will can
be billed by creditors for up to at least a year after you die.

Estate taxes: Assets transferred through a pour-over will
are considered part of your taxable estate. If, when these are
added to your other taxable assets, including those in a
revocable living trust, your estate totals more than $600,000,
it will be subject to a sizable federal estate tax.

Avoiding these disadvantages is likely to be the very reason you chose to set up a living trust in the first place. That's
why it's best to place as many assets as you can into your
living trust, which you can change with relative ease, and
leave as little as possible to the pour-over will.

EXAMPLE

When Phil, a bachelor, died unexpectedly, his sister Suzanne
discovered he had forgotten to place 1,000 shares of recently
acquired stock into his revocable living trust. Suzanne had to
pay an attorney several thousand dollars to usher it through
probate. This would have been true regardless of whether or
not his will had included a pour-over clause. By including such
a provision in his will, however, Phil assured that his trust
beneficiary—a favorite nephew—would inherit a special
share of the stock's remaining value.

CHAPTER 12

TESTAMENTARY TRUSTS

Testamentary trusts, also known as *will trusts* or *court trusts,* are created in your will and do not take effect (come into action) until you die. Unlike a living trust, which is set up primarily to avoid probate and usually distributes the grantor's assets shortly after death, the testamentary trust does not avoid probate and usually lasts a long time after the grantor dies.

You might choose to set up a testamentary trust for any of a number of reasons, mostly long term. These include:

- To control how quickly and when your property is spent; instead of giving your heirs single, lump-sum gifts as an ordinary will might, a testamentary trust can provide a variety of other options, including periodic income on a schedule you set up in the trust
- To make sure a capable person is managing your assets for a dependent family member, spouse or minor child when you die
- To protect your property from the spendthrift actions of a beneficiary
- To protect the inheritance from problems beneficiaries may encounter, such as divorce, lawsuits or Medicaid requirements
- To provide for a grandchild's education
- To reduce or eliminate federal estate taxes

Some or all of these goals could also be accomplished by a living trust, of course, but those who choose to set up a testamentary trust instead usually have another objective they want to achieve that makes living trusts unattractive:

- To avoid the immediate expense and trouble of creating and maintaining a living trust but to allow their heirs to benefit from the asset management and tax benefits a trust can give

Anyone can be named beneficiary of a testamentary trust, but the most commonly designated are spouses, children and grandchildren. Trusts for spouses are discussed in Chapter 13, those for children in Chapter 14. The remainder of this chapter provides an overview of the advantages and disadvantages of writing a trust into your will and how to go about doing so.

Technically speaking, testamentary trusts are irrevocable: Once they're created, you don't get to change or cancel them because, legally, they don't come into existence until after you die and your estate is probated. Of course, you can change the trust's terms or even cancel it entirely any time during your life simply by rewriting your will. The law doesn't consider this amending or revoking the trust because the trust isn't considered to exist yet.

EXAMPLE

Laura and Al, an ailing couple in their 70s, want to encourage their three grandchildren to continue their education past high school. However, they don't want to relinquish their assets until they die. They decide to write into their will a testamentary trust for their grandchildren. In it, instead of turning the assets over to the four grandchildren in a lump sum, they bequeath their home to the trust and instruct the trust to sell it and use the proceeds to pay for any schooling past high school that the children choose to pursue. Two years later, when one of the grandchildren dies in an auto accident, they rewrite their will to eliminate that grandchild from the trust.

When both Laura and Al have died, the house goes through probate and is taxed along with the other assets in their estate. After that, the house is turned over to the trust.

Advantages

As with other trusts, a testamentary trust provides continuing care for your family and other beneficiaries after you've died. It can be used to support your spouse, educate your children or grandchildren, care for a sick relative—whatever you instruct it to do, for as long as the assets last and providing it's legal.

Asset management: A testamentary trust allows you to name a trustee to manage the assets for your beneficiaries instead of turning over to those beneficiaries their lump-sum inheritances.

Estate taxes: Although you must pay estate taxes on any money from your estate that's used to fund your testamentary trust, the primary purpose for setting up a testamentary trust is often to avoid a second estate tax bite, the one paid by either your surviving spouse or your children. See Chapters 13 and 14 for information on bypass and generation-skipping trusts.

Probate: Although assets used to fund a testamentary trust must go through probate when you die, an especially advantageous use of a testamentary trust is to benefit your spouse so that the assets don't go through probate a second time when the surviving spouse dies. Without a testamentary trust, any assets the first spouse leaves to the survivor have to be probated twice—once when each spouse dies.

Income: Because your testamentary trust doesn't take effect until you die, you continue to enjoy all of your assets as long as you live. Testamentary trusts often include a provision for lifetime income to one beneficiary (for example, your spouse) and the remainder to one or more others (such as your children).

Spendthrift provision: A clause protecting your assets

from a financially unsophisticated beneficiary or a beneficiary's creditors can be included.

Complexity: A testamentary trust is usually easier to create than a living trust and does not involve title transfers.

Disadvantages

Testamentary trusts have a number of disadvantages as
well:

Estate taxes: Although these trusts can help your heirs
avoid these taxes, they have no effect on the federal estate
taxes you owe. This is because, as explained before, the trust
is funded with after-tax dollars. That means the trust is not
funded until your estate is settled and the taxes you owe are
paid.

Probate: Although the trust can help you avoid double
probate (see above and Chapters 13 and 14), the trust assets
do have to be probated before being turned over to the
trust. This can mean major delays in distributing those assets
to the beneficiaries and even more monetary outlays, this
time for lawyers and court fees. Moreover, a testamentary
trust continues under the supervision of the court system,
normally with required periodic reviews or approvals and
more complications and expenses when changing trustees.

Income taxes: Testamentary trusts won't save on your
income taxes; for that you need an irrevocable living trust.
With a testamentary trust, you're obligated to pay taxes on
whatever income your assets generate because you continue to own and manage those assets until you die.

Creditors' claims: Any assets left in your will, including
those intended for a trust, can be billed by your creditors up
to at least a year after you die.

TYPICAL CLAUSES

To create a testamentary trust, you simply draft a will that meets the execution requirements for a valid will in your state and include a clause or provision that creates the trust and identifies the assets you want placed into it. Be sure to include:

- Your name and place of residence
- A statement revoking all prior wills (because this trust is created in your new will)
- The name(s) of guardian(s) for minor(s)
- The name(s) of executor(s), trustee(s) and successor trustee(s)
- The names of beneficiaries and alternate beneficiaries
- Bond requirements, if any
- Instructions for paying taxes and funeral costs
- A description of the assets you're leaving immediately
- A description of the assets you're placing into the trust
- When and how the assets should be distributed
- Instructions about what is to happen if a beneficiary dies before you or before the assets are distributed
- The powers of the executor(s) and the trustee(s)
- Your signature
- The date the will is executed
- Signatures and a statement by witnesses (two or three, depending on the laws of the state in which you live)
- The signature and seal of a notary public

PART IV

SPECIAL-PURPOSE TRUSTS

CHAPTER 13

MARITAL TRUSTS

The primary goal of marital trusts is not, as you might expect, to get the best tax and probate advantage when you leave your assets to your spouse, but to pass along to your children or other heirs as much of your estate as possible free of federal estate taxes. These trusts are of practical value only to married people whose combined assets are worth more than $600,000, because federal estate taxes aren't assessed against estates worth less than that. As discussed in Chapter 5, when you leave everything unconditionally to your spouse, the unlimited marital deduction exempts those assets from federal estate taxes anyway, whether you leave them to your spouse in a will, a trust, a life insurance policy or any other way. Marital trusts allow you to keep the tax advantage of that marital deduction while naming someone other than your spouse—a child from a previous marriage, for example—as the ultimate beneficiary of an asset.

Even if you want to pass all your assets on to your spouse unconditionally when you die, you should consider whether that's necessary or wise: The marital deduction can lead to a tax trap later on. If, as a result of the money you passed tax free to your spouse, you push your spouse's total estate above the $600,000 federal exemption ceiling, that estate will have to pay a large federal tax when your spouse dies. Instead of the two of you passing along $1.2 million to your heirs tax free, only $600,000 of your combined estate will be exempt. In effect, you will have failed to take advantage of your own $600,000 federal tax exemption by passing your assets directly on to your spouse.

To ensure that you take full advantage of both your federal tax exemption *and* the unlimited marital deduction, you can set up one trust or a package of trusts. Each trust in your package can be designed to meet specific needs. A couple with millions of dollars worth of assets typically will set up a trust plan that includes three, four or even five trusts, depending how much control they want the surviving spouse to have over each asset. Each trust in the plan directs who is to be the ultimate beneficiary of the trust's assets. The package may even include a special trust for children (see Chapter 14).

Marital trusts can be either testamentary (created in your will) or living. It really depends on whether you want the trust to go into effect before or after you die.

The two most popular trusts that spouses create are the *bypass trust* and the *qualified terminable interest property (QTIP) trust.* The bypass trust is not technically a marital trust because it is not set up to take advantage of the marital deduction; instead, its purpose is to ensure that you preserve your $600,000 federal tax exemption. Nevertheless, it is included in this chapter because it is typically set up together with a married couple's estate plan.

As described below, both bypass and QTIP trusts have strict restrictions on what your spouse can do with the money you put into the trust. *Power-of-appointment* (POA) *trusts* do not have such restrictions. A POA trust gives your spouse unlimited access to the trust principal, but, as we will see, it sacrifices the tax advantages you gain in exchange for fewer restrictions.

If you talk to a trust specialist, you'll probably also hear about something called an A–B trust. This is merely a combination of a QTIP and a bypass trust. In fact, most marital trust plans are combinations of the three trusts described in this chapter: bypass, QTIP and POA.

One note of caution before we discuss the general guidelines and strategies of the three types of trusts: If you are planning to set up one or more of these trusts, you should consult a professional. These trusts can have serious financial, business, tax and even personal implications. Also, the three basic trusts we describe have so many possible permutations, they are best understood in relation to your particular assets and estate-planning goals.

BYPASS TRUSTS

If a married couple's assets exceed $600,000, they should seriously consider establishing a bypass trust to ensure that they get full advantage of each spouse's $600,000 federal estate tax exemption. Trust specialists have a number of names for this kind of trust: *residuary trust, family trust, Trust B, credit shelter trust* and *nonmarital trust.*

We use the term "bypass" because it best conveys what the trust does. The basic idea is that, upon your death, your spouse (or anyone else you wish to name) gets some or all of the income earned by the tax-exempt $600,000 you put into the trust, but when the survivor dies, the $600,000 trust principal passes directly to one or more other beneficiaries, usually your children, without being subject to federal taxes or probate.

The catch is that your spouse must give up almost all ownership rights over the $600,000 you put in the bypass trust. The income may go to the survivor, but your spouse cannot "invade" the trust principal except for certain limited reasons, such as health care or basic survival needs. The payoff for giving up the surviving spouse's access to the trust principal is that your beneficiaries will owe less in federal estate taxes and you get more control over the ultimate distribution of the assets.

Let's assume you die before your spouse. The assets you put into a bypass trust are included in your estate and are taxed when you die. However, because $600,000 of your estate is exempt from federal estate taxes, the $600,000 in the trust incurs no federal estate tax. (If the bypass trust was set up as a living trust and not as a testamentary trust, the $600,000 would also escape probate.) When your spouse dies, the money in the trust is again not included in the taxable estate because your spouse's ownership of it was limited. Therefore, the assets "bypass" a second tax bite and probate and go directly to your trust beneficiaries.

In some circumstances, you might decide to put more than $600,000 into a bypass trust. Although the amount above $600,000 will be taxed at your death, the overall final estate tax may be less than if these assets were added to and taxed with your surviving spouse's assets. This is called *estate equalization* and is based on the principle that two taxes on 50 percent of the estate each can amount to less than one tax on 100 percent of the estate because the tax rate is lower for smaller estates.

EXAMPLE

Max, whose assets total $800,000, creates an estate plan that will put $600,000 of his assets into a bypass trust when he dies and pass the rest unconditionally to his wife, Simone. When Max dies, $600,000 goes into the bypass trust, with his wife as income beneficiary and his son Buster as beneficiary of the remainder. He gives his remaining $200,000 unconditionally to Simone. No federal estate tax is due at Max's death because the $600,000 placed in the trust qualifies for the federal estate tax exemption and the remainder passes tax free to Simone under the unlimited marital deduction.

Simone, who has $400,000 of her own assets, receives income from the bypass trust for life, but she cannot touch the $600,000 principal unless the trustee agrees that she needs the money for a medical emergency or basic survival. When Simone dies, the $600,000 in the trust goes directly to Buster. Because Simone's own assets now also total $600,000—Max's $200,000 plus her own $400,000—no federal estate tax is owed on her estate either, because she gets her personal $600,000 federal exemption.

If, instead of creating a bypass trust, Max had used the unlimited marital deduction to give his entire $800,000 to Simone, federal estate taxes would have to be paid when she died because her estate—Max's $800,000 and her $400,000— would total $1.2 million. After her exemption of $600,000, her estate would owe $235,000 in taxes on the remaining $600,000. In addition, Simone would have total control over who would receive the estate—Buster or someone else.

For older couples with substantial assets, a bypass trust is a standard estate-planning tool, but it may not be practical for young couples, because with this trust, when one spouse dies the surviving spouse has only limited access to the trust assets. A young surviving spouse, especially one with family responsibilities, is likely to need access to the full marital estate.

QTIP TRUSTS

A qualified terminable interest property trust, commonly called a "QTIP trust," is the most popular marital trust today. It is used to make the most of the unlimited marital tax deduction while allowing you to control who gets the assets after your surviving spouse dies. With a QTIP trust, after you die, estate taxes are not owed until your spouse dies. This keeps more trust assets working to generate income while your spouse is alive. Of course, the IRS will insist that these assets be included in your surviving spouse's estate and be subject to federal estate tax before they are passed on to their ultimate beneficiary.

To ensure that your trust qualifies for the unlimited marital deduction, a QTIP trust must include certain provisions. Most important, the surviving spouse must be paid all income earned on the trust assets each year. Unlike a bypass trust, which allows you to assign the interest income to anyone, you *must* make your spouse the income beneficiary of the QTIP trust and its *only* income beneficiary. This prevents the surviving spouse from paying income tax at a lower tax rate. Your spouse is not even allowed to give away this income so that taxes are paid by someone in a lower tax bracket.

Another requirement of the QTIP trust is that no one be given authority to give any part of the trust assets away to someone else—including to the surviving spouse or the trustee—during the surviving spouse's life. This ensures that these assets, which were passed on tax free to the surviving spouse, will be included in the spouse's estate for federal estate taxes when that spouse dies. The result is that taxes will be paid on any of the couple's assets that are left at the second spouse's death.

EXAMPLE

Andrew and Theresa, a married couple with $2 million in assets, set up three trusts. When Andrew dies at age 80, $600,000 of his assets go into Trust B—a bypass trust—and his remaining $400,000 goes into Trust C—a QTIP trust. No federal estate taxes are paid: The exemption shields the $600,000 in Trust B and the QTIP shields the remainder—for now. Theresa's half of their assets (the other $1 million) goes into a living trust, Trust A. Theresa continues to live in the couple's home and collects income from all three trusts. She may cancel or change Trust A any time, but not Trusts B or C, and she may not "invade" the principal in either Trust B or Trust C. When she dies 10 years later, her estate must pay taxes on $400,000 of her original $1 million (the worth above her $600,000 federal exemption) and on the $400,000 in Trust C. Thus, the couple has preserved both $600,000 exemptions.

Who uses QTIP trusts? Most often, wealthy people who have children from a previous marriage. They use income generated by the trust to support a surviving spouse for life and, when that spouse dies, pass the remaining assets (both the income and the principal) to whomever the grantor designates. Frequently, these ultimate beneficiaries are children from an earlier marriage.

POWER-OF-APPOINTMENT (POA) TRUSTS

General power-of-appointment (POA) trusts, also known as *marital deduction trusts,* are used less frequently today because they do not give the grantor control over who ultimately inherits the assets put into the trust. In fact, they differ very little from taking direct advantage of the marital deduction simply by giving your assets to your spouse. A POA trust gives the surviving spouse an absolute right to dispose of the trust assets—either the principal or the income—when the surviving spouse dies, sometimes even during life. Also, unlike a QTIP trust, the POA can give the surviving spouse authority to use the principal in the trust for others, subject to gift tax rules. Because the surviving spouse has such complete control over the trust assets, all POA trust assets are included in the surviving spouse's taxable estate, just as if an outright bequest had been made.

If the trust and its assets are left untouched by the surviving spouse, the assets go to the heir designated in the trust document before the first spouse died. Thus, POA trusts can be thought of as acts of faith: They are usually created with the hope that the surviving spouse will not exercise his or her rights under the trust and that the trust will remain untouched.

Like the QTIP trust, a POA trust is used in combination with a bypass trust. Sometimes, one asset is owned partly by one trust and partly by the other. Again, if any of these variations and combinations interests you, you should talk with a professional estate planner.

Advantages

Estate taxes: As we've seen, the bypass trust offers significant federal estate tax advantages while the QTIP and POA trusts do not. These latter two trusts do, however, delay the federal estate tax that has to be paid on your assets until both spouses have died. Of course, this can also be accomplished by an outright gift or bequest of the assets to your spouse.

Probate: Assets in each of the trusts are not considered part of the surviving spouse's estate. After the second spouse dies, they pass directly to the beneficiaries named in the trusts, without going through probate.

Income: All three trusts can be used to provide the surviving spouse with income as long as she or he lives. However, the QTIP and POA trusts require that the spouse be paid this income as it is earned, while under a bypass trust the surviving spouse need not be the only income beneficiary and isn't even obliged to collect any income from the trust.

Asset management: Any trustee can be named to manage the assets, although with what's known as a lifetime-withdrawal POA, the surviving spouse can cancel the trust or otherwise intervene in asset management plans at any time.

Other: Creating a bypass trust can sometimes allow the surviving spouse to receive government health benefits, such as Medicaid, without first having to exhaust the trust's assets to qualify. If one of your goals is to protect your assets and still remain eligible for government benefits, you should seek professional help. See also "Medicaid Qualifying Trusts" in Chapter 17.

Disadvantages

Flexibility: The major drawback to the bypass and QTIP trusts is their lack of flexibility after they become irrevocable. Unless the surviving spouse is given a limited power of appointment, the terms can't be changed and neither trust can be canceled by the surviving spouse.

Control: With both the bypass and most QTIP trusts, the surviving spouse is not allowed to touch the trust principal except to pay for specific medical expenses and basic survival needs.

Income taxes: Income taxes are owed on all income received from the trusts and are paid either by the trust or, if they are distributed, by the beneficiary. As both the QTIP and POA trusts require that the surviving spouse receive the income the trust earns each year, this can have a substantial impact on the income taxes owed by larger estates. Various strategies are available for lowering income taxes, and you should consult a professional to learn about your options.

Complexity: These trusts come in many variations and with many other considerations. Again, you should consult a professional before setting up any such trust plan—and be prepared to pay for the advice and help you get.

CHAPTER 14

TRUSTS FOR CHILDREN

Many parents think the only reason to set up a trust for their children is to make sure that they're cared for and their education is provided for if the parents die before the children reach adulthood. Although some trusts do just that, many trusts for children are also used to lower parents' taxable income and to reduce taxes on their heirs' estates. Recent tax law changes have reduced how much you can save by stashing income in trusts for your children, but such trusts still allow you to save a significant amount over the years.

You don't have to be wealthy to benefit from creating a child's trust, but most people don't create one unless they have at least $25,000 to fund it. That's because a child's trust can be costly to draft and manage: It's usually more complex than a simple living trust and often has a longer life.

You don't even have to be a parent to create a trust for a child. Grandparents, uncles, aunts and friends all can and do set up such trusts.

A child's trust may be written into a will and activated when you die (testamentary), but if it is, the assets will have to pass through probate. That's why most people choose instead to create living trusts for their children. These may be either revocable or irrevocable. They may also be made as separate trusts or as part of a larger, broader-purpose living trust. Creating a living trust guarantees that your assets won't go through probate. If the trust is irrevocable, it can also lower your taxable income and eliminate estate taxes when you die.

GENERAL PROVISIONS

Parents can either be the trustees of their own children's trusts or, if tax considerations are involved, name someone else—a relative, a friend, even a bank. If you're the trustee, be certain to name a successor trustee to serve if you die before the trust terminates. You might want to name your children's guardian as your successor trustee, which will simplify management of the child's resources when you die.

A trust for a child must contain at least this information:

- How long the trust is to pay income to the child
- At what age the child should receive the remaining trust assets
- Under what conditions the trustee may use the assets to pay for the child's education and welfare
- The name of a successor trustee to manage the trust if the original trustee dies or is unable to serve
- The name of a guardian to care for the child if you die before he or she becomes an adult
- What is to happen to the assets if the child dies before the trust expires

You may also want to include a spendthrift provision instructing the trustee when and how much income should be paid to beneficiaries who are too young to make financial decisions for themselves. Such a provision might forbid that trust assets be spent based on an expectation of income from the trust. For example, a child couldn't buy a car and expect the trust to pay for it.

You can instruct that the trust hold the assets for the child's entire life, although most people instruct the trust to turn the assets over when the child reaches a responsible age—typically 25 to 30 years old.

Finally, remember to review the trust for needed revision whenever a child is born, adopted or dies to be sure the document still reflects your family's needs.

The remainder of this chapter discusses four trusts designed specifically for children.

SECTION 2503(C) TRUSTS

One popular child's trust is the Section 2503(c) trust, named for the section of the Internal Revenue Code that governs it. A Section 2503(c) trust allows you to place up to $10,000 a year in a trust for a minor child without incurring a gift tax.

As mentioned in Chapter 5, you can give up to $10,000 a year per person (a couple can give up to $20,000 a year) to each of any number of individuals for birthdays, graduation or other uses without paying gift taxes, as long as the person receiving the money has immediate access to it.

Although it's legal, giving $10,000 a year to a minor child to gain tax benefits is, of course, impractical and even irresponsible. The IRS therefore allows parents to create a Section 2503(c) trust for any child under 21 years old. Parents can fund the trust each year without incurring a gift tax as long as their contributions are $10,000 or less and their trust does the following:

- Allows the trustee to spend some or all of the trust property for the child's benefit before the child turns 21
- Distributes the remaining trust property to the child when the child turns 21
- Instructs the trustee to pay assets and accumulated income to the child's estate, or as the child may direct, or

as the parent specifies, or if the child dies before turning 21

Typically, trusts are designed to end and distribute its assets to beneficiaries when they reach the age of 21, the age when most people are considered capable of handling their own financial affairs. The trust may, however, continue longer than that if the parents include in it what is known as a Crummey provision (see Chapter 15). This gives the child a window (typically 30 days after turning 21) in which to collect all of the trust's assets and end the trust. If the child doesn't take advantage of this within the time limit, the trust may continue to whatever age is specified in the trust.

No restrictions apply to the type of assets that can be transferred to a Section 2503(c) trust, but some other restrictions are imposed:

- Any amount may be put into the trust, but amounts above $10,000 transferred to the trust during any one year will not qualify for the gift tax exclusion.
- A separate Section 2503(c) trust must be set up for each child. You may not provide for several children in a single trust.
- The trust must be irrevocable—it may not be changed or canceled.
- The trust may be created only after the child is born. You may not, for example, create a 2503(c) trust for your daughter's unborn child.

EXAMPLE

Marty and Richard, who are in the 33 percent income tax bracket, set up a Section 2503(c) trust for their daughter, Katie, when she is 4 years old. They fund it with $10,000 a year and instruct the trustee to pay Katie $1,000 in interest income each year until she turns 21, then to turn the remaining assets over to her. Marty and Richard will pay no income tax on the money they put into the trust or the income generated by trust assets, except for the $1,000 income Katie receives each year. That $1,000 will be taxed at Katie's tax rate until she turns 14. (If Katie's investment income from all her sources—her trust, bank account or other source—exceeds $1,000, the excess will be taxed at her parents' rate; see Chapter 5.) After Katie turns 14, all her income is taxed at her own tax rate, which is probably lower than her parents'.

Advantages

Section 2503(c) trusts offer these advantages:

Gift tax: It allows you to fund the trust with contributions of up to $10,000 each year without paying a gift tax.

Asset management: It allows the trust assets to be managed and distributed according to your wishes until your child or grandchild turns 21.

Income: It can provide your child or grandchild with income for clothing, education or whatever other needs the child has.

Disadvantages

Section 2503(c) trusts also have a number of disadvantages:

Irrevocability: The trust is irrevocable; you may not change beneficiaries, instructions or assets, and you may not cancel the trust.

Income taxes: Although the money you put into the trust isn't taxable and the income the trust generates may not be taxable to you, all distributions to your child or grandchild above $1,000 a year are taxed at your tax rate until the child turns 14. If the trust extends past the beneficiary's 21st birthday, the child is considered its legal owner and must pay taxes on the income the trust generates, whether the child collects the income or not and whether or not you include a Crummey provision (see Chapter 15) in the trust document.

Trustee: For estate tax savings, you must not serve as trustee for any assets you give to the trust.

Complexity: In general, it's wise to be careful and get professional advice when setting up a Section 2503(c) trust. Because it's irrevocable, once it's created you won't be able to undo it. Be sure that you want your child or grandchild to have the trust assets at age 21 (or any later age you designate if you include a Crummey provision) and that you feel comfortable that the child will be able to manage those assets when they are turned over. If your answer to either question is no, you may be better off using some other form of trust.

Also, remember that you must create a separate trust for each beneficiary. This could be costly if you hire a professional to do the work and have several children or grandchildren to provide for. It could also be time consuming if you decide to do it yourself.

GENERATION-SKIPPING TRUSTS

If you're wealthy, you can use a generation-skipping trust to transfer up to $1 million in assets to your grandchildren without their having to pay federal estate taxes on the money when their parent—your child—dies.

You can "skip" a generation of federal estate taxes by setting up a trust that pays income to your children for life and afterwards distributes the trust's assets to your grandchildren. Because your children never own the assets you placed in the trust, those assets may not be included in the estate the federal government will tax.

As of 1986, an individual can place up to $1 million in assets in a generation-skipping trust without incurring a generation-skipping transfer tax. If you know you want to pass that much on to your grandchildren and know your children will benefit enough from receiving income from that $1 million but not need the $1 million itself, you should probably consider setting up a generation-skipping trust.

You can use any of several distribution schemes. You might instruct the trustee to pay each grandchild his or her share of the trust assets when the youngest grandchild reaches a certain age, say 21. You might instruct the trustee to distribute the assets to each grandchild as he or she reaches a certain age; the assets would therefore be distributed at different times. Or the trust assets might be distributed to the grandchildren when your youngest child dies. (This last option isn't as popular as the others as it means that the grandchildren may have to wait a long time to get their inheritances, possibly until they themselves are well established financially, or even retired.)

A generation-skipping trust can be either living or testamentary (written into a will). Most people create generation-skipping trusts in their will. Of course, the drawback to this is that the assets must pass through probate.

EXAMPLE

Sarah, a 68-year-old widow, has two children and four grandchildren. She owns a number of valuable assets—$5 million in property, her jewelry, her late husband's Civil War gun collection, two cars and other personal property. Her two children inherited $2 million each when her husband died, and she wants to make sure that her grandchildren receive her assets but doesn't want those assets depleted by the hefty estate taxes that would be due on her children's estates if she were to leave her assets to them directly. She leaves some of her estate to charity and creates a generation-skipping trust in her will for her grandchildren. When she dies, her children receive income from her trust assets but may not touch the assets themselves. She instructs the trustee to give each grandchild his or her inheritance at age 35. Had Sarah not created the trust, her estate would have passed first to her children, and substantial federal estate taxes would have had to be paid as each of her children died.

Advantages

Estate taxes: The biggest benefit of a generation-skipping trust is that it reduces the total estate taxes a family has to pay, as demonstrated by the example above. This is of major importance to estates worth more than the federally exempt level.

If you leave your assets to your children in a will without such a trust, the money will be taxed twice—once when you die, again when they die (unless they've spent the assets, of course). Using a generation-skipping trust, $1 million of your assets "skips" one generation of taxation.

Asset management: Most people name their children as trustees of a generation-skipping trust, so they can exercise some control over how the assets are managed and distributed to their own children.

Income: The trust's principal and any income it generates can be earmarked for the support and education of your grandchildren.

Disadvantages

Income: Although your children can receive income for life from your trust, they may not get to its principal except in limited circumstances.

Probate: If the trust is set up in a will, as many are, the assets will be subject to the delays and expense of probate before being turned over to the trust.

Complexity: It's best to seek professional advice when setting up a generation-skipping trust. Because the trust is designed to last a long time—at least two generations—careful drafting is essential so the rule against perpetuities isn't violated. Also, the potential of unforeseen events (birth, death, serious illness, bankruptcy) should inspire caution before creating such a trust.

FAMILY POT TRUSTS

The family pot trust pools your assets in a common trust for your children. Unlike other children's trusts, it lets your trustee distribute income to each beneficiary based on his or her individual need.

The family pot trust is used primarily to support and educate your children, but it may be used for other reasons. It ends when the youngest beneficiary reaches whatever age you specify in the document—usually 21. When the last child reaches the age you specify, the trust's principal and income are distributed equally among all of the children. As with many other trusts discussed in this book, the family pot trust can be either a living trust (created while you are alive) or a testamentary trust (created in your will). Because parents want to continue managing their money for their children, they usually create a family pot trust to take effect after they die.

Advantages
Income and asset management: The major advantage of this trust is that it gives the trustee freedom to distribute funds based on each beneficiary's needs.

Disadvantages
The family pot trust has a number of disadvantages:

Asset management: Freedom is a double-edged sword. Because the trust gives your trustee broad latitude in how to distribute the assets, the trustee may show preference to one child over another in a way you would not approve of. Once you die, you will have no control over how the assets are disbursed.

Another limitation is that a child can't receive his or her share of the principal until the youngest beneficiary reaches the age you specify. If your children aren't close to one another in age, some may be in their thirties or forties before they can receive the bulk of their inheritance.

Complexity: A family pot trust requires fairly complex tax forms; a professional should be consulted.

Probate: If the trust is created in your will, its assets will have to be probated.

EDUCATIONAL TRUSTS

You can set up a trust specifically to pay for a child's education. An educational trust can do more than that, however. It also can reduce your income taxes.

The trust can shift income earned on your assets from your tax bracket to that of a child's or grandchild's in a lower tax bracket as long as that child has reached age 14. Thus, the trust is far more advantageous when supporting the education of children who have reached high school age, much less so for supporting elementary school education. To get the tax advantages, educational trusts must be both living and irrevocable, and you may not be the trustee.

EXAMPLE

When their daughter Lauren is 12, Linda and Steve put $250,000 into an educational trust to pay for her private schooling from age 14 until she completes college and any graduate education she chooses to undertake. Louise, Lauren's aunt, acts as trustee and pays Lauren's tuition and other educational expenses from the trust income. Lauren is taxed at her parents' rate, 33 percent, on the trust money she receives until she turns 14, except for the first $1,000, which is taxed at her rate. After that, she pays taxes based on her own income from both the trust and other sources. Because that income totals less than $15,000 each year, the money is taxed at the lowest rate—15 percent—while she's in school.

Advantages

Probate: Because it's a living trust, the trust assets are not subject to the delays or expense of probate.

Estate taxes: Your estate taxes, if any, are reduced or eliminated because the value of your estate is reduced by the amount you put into the trust.

Income taxes: Because you no longer control the assets or receive income generated by those assets (the trust does), your personal income taxes are reduced.

Disadvantages

Despite their benefits, educational trusts also carry a number of disadvantages:

Asset management: You must surrender control of the assets by appointing someone else as trustee.

Irrevocability: You give up the right to change or cancel the trust.

Income: You may not receive any income from the trust.

Income taxes: You probably can't guarantee that your children will be in a lower tax bracket when you die than you were during the lifetime of the trust. If they are in the same tax bracket or a higher one when they collect income from the trust assets, no income tax will have been saved.

Complexity: Tax laws governing irrevocable living trusts are fairly complex, so before creating such a trust, consider seeking professional estate-planning advice.

CHAPTER 15

INSURANCE TRUSTS

People usually buy life insurance to provide financial security for their loved ones after they die. Traditionally, this means naming one or more beneficiaries on the policy to collect the insurance proceeds in a single payment after your death. The beneficiary gets the money promptly, without the delay and expense of probate. From this insurance money, the beneficiary typically pays funeral expenses, final medical bills and any debts you left behind.

However, with this arrangement, the value of these insurance proceeds will be considered part of your estate for federal tax purposes. If the value of your estate exceeds or is approaching $600,000, or if you have an insurance policy large enough to push your estate's total value above that amount, it could mean the difference between paying no federal estate tax and having a substantial amount of your estate gobbled up by the tax collector. (If you have named your spouse as beneficiary of your insurance, then the money will pass tax free under the unlimited marital deduction, but this could simply postpone the tax bite by increasing your spouse's eventual estate beyond the exemption ceiling.)

What's more, if you don't name a beneficiary on your life insurance policy, or if your beneficiary dies before you do, the money the policy pays out will become part of your estate, subject not only to taxation but also to probate. In other words, your estate will inherit the money and it then will have to go through the trouble, delay and expense of probate. Probate could well delay receipt of your insurance benefits a year or more.

If you don't want to name a beneficiary on your policy but want to avoid probate, if you want to pass life insurance proceeds on to loved ones without federal estate taxes, or if you want the proceeds distributed in periodic payments rather than one lump sum, you should consider setting up an irrevocable insurance trust or adding your insurance policy to an existing trust.

An irrevocable insurance trust, in particular, will keep the proceeds out of your estate for tax and probate purposes and give you flexibility as to how and when the benefits will be paid out after you die.

Because you transfer ownership of the insurance policy to the trust, you no longer own the policy; the trust does. Therefore, the insurance proceeds are no longer considered part of your estate when federal estate taxes are calculated. However, to get the tax advantages, you must live at least three years after the transfer of an existing policy to an insurance trust. Also, to make sure the value of the policy is removed from your taxable estate, you must give up all incidents of ownership over the policy, including the right to change the beneficiary, the right to borrow against the policy and the right to cancel the trust. And, as mentioned in the discussion of irrevocable living trusts in Chapter 10, you may not be the trustee or the beneficiary.

The safest way to ensure that you have given up all ownership rights is to have your trustee buy a new insurance policy for you and transfer it to a trust. The trustee will name you as the insured and the trust as the beneficiary. When you die, the insurance company will release the proceeds to your trustee, who will then distribute those proceeds to your beneficiaries, free of federal estate taxes and probate. The tricky part is that you must supply the trustee with money to pay the insurance premiums, and if you don't do it correctly, you could end up owing gift taxes on your own insurance payments. The *Crummey provision* now comes into play.

THE CRUMMEY PROVISION

Regardless of what kind of insurance trust you create, you'll owe gift taxes on the premiums you pay to the insurance company, because in effect those payments are a "gift" to your trust. This means your premium payments will lower your $600,000 tax credit (see Chapter 5) and possibly increase your federal estate taxes. Further, these premiums are not even considered exempt from tax under the $10,000-per-person annual gift tax exemption because they are considered a gift of a *future interest.* Only "present" gifts are considered gifts under the annual tax-exemption rules.

You can avoid this gift tax, however, if you include a Crummey provision in your insurance trust. The name has nothing to do with either a lack of desirability or granular qualities. It is named after the person who successfully sued to use it. This provision allows you to give up to $10,000 a year to each beneficiary of your insurance trust, but instead of giving the money directly to each beneficiary, you give it to the trustee. The trustee, in turn, notifies the beneficiaries about the gift and tells them that unless they collect on it, the money will be used to pay the premium on the trust insurance policy. (Actually, a Crummey provision can be used in any trust that bestows a future interest to convert it to a *present interest* so gift taxes are avoided.)

You can't stop your beneficiaries from making withdrawals under this provision; hence you have created a "present," not a "future," interest. Because you created the present interest, you are considered to have made a gift and can take advantage of the $10,000-per-person annual gift tax exclusion. Just be sure your beneficiaries understand they're not to take you up on this present "gift," that their best interest lies in letting the money be used to pay for the insurance they'll eventually collect. With most beneficiaries, you probably won't have any problems.

Setting up an insurance trust doesn't prevent you from instructing your family to use part of the insurance money to pay funeral expenses and debts—as with trusts generally, it adds great flexibility. You can draw up a plan for distributing the benefits to your spouse and children over time according to a schedule you set up, or at the discretion of your trustee. You can also instruct the trust to pay out the insurance money in a lump sum, just as would be the case if you named the beneficiaries on the policy itself. You can even name your spouse as the trustee. Here are two examples of how an insurance trust might work.

EXAMPLE

Sally named her daughter the beneficiary of her $250,000 life insurance policy. She didn't name her son as a beneficiary because it appeared at the time that he would be independently well off. Now the tables have turned, and her son needs the money far more than her daughter does. Recognizing that fortunes rise and fall and that she cannot be assured which of them will need the insurance money most, Sally transfers ownership of the policy to an irrevocable insurance trust and names her brother as trustee. She instructs the trust to distribute the assets in annual payments according to the need of each child. When her son reaches 30, the trust is to distribute any remaining funds to the two children, again based on need. The trust comes into existence when Sally creates it but will not be fully funded until she dies. The insurance money will not have to go through probate, and if she lives at least three years after the policy is transferred to the trust, it will not be added to her taxable estate.

EXAMPLE

David has a $500,000 life insurance policy and names as owner and beneficiary the irrevocable living trust he created five years ago. The trust already includes instructions to pay his funeral expenses and debts, including final medical expenses, from its assets. His niece will receive $400,000 of the after-expenses trust money in a lump sum when she reaches age 25, and the remainder of the assets will then be distributed in equal portions to any other nieces and nephews living at that time. When David dies, the $500,000 in insurance money is not probated or subject to estate tax, even though adding the insurance money to his other assets increases his estate well beyond the $600,000 that is federally exempt from taxation.

GENERAL PROVISIONS

You may name any of the following types of trusts as beneficiary of your life insurance:

- An irrevocable living trust, which takes effect during your life but may not be changed or canceled (some states prohibit this kind of insurance trust, however)
- A revocable living trust, which takes effect during your life and may be changed or canceled
- A testamentary trust, which is created by your will and takes effect after you die

Any type of life insurance can be placed into the trust. You can buy a new policy and place it into an insurance trust or transfer an existing policy to the trust. Insurance provided by an employer sometimes can't be transferred to an irrevo-cable trust because many employer-provided policies include a provision that the employee may change the beneficiary. If you want to have your employer-provided policy included, you should have your employer notify the insurance company that you name your irrevocable trust as the policy's beneficiary and that you give up the right ever to change the beneficiary again.

IRREVOCABLE INSURANCE TRUSTS

Advantages

Probate: The irrevocable insurance trust avoids probate.

Estate taxes: Unlike the revocable insurance trust, the irrevocable variety can protect your insurance benefits from estate taxes. This is the primary reason many people create this kind of trust. If your estate is approaching or is already worth the federally exempt $600,000, you may want to create a separate, irrevocable living trust for your life insurance to complement your revocable trust, simply to keep the insurance assets out of your taxable estate. For your insurance proceeds to benefit from this tax advantage, however, you must give the policy to the trust at least three years before you die, or the trustee must purchase the policy for the trust.

Disadvantages

Irrevocability: Once you create the trust, you give up complete control of it and the insurance policies. That's the trade you make for the tax and other benefits. You may not change the beneficiaries, and you may not name yourself the trustee.

EXAMPLE

Sam has $1.5 million in assets. He creates two trusts—a revocable living trust for $1 million and an irrevocable insurance trust with his life insurance policies, worth $500,000. As circumstances change from time to time, he changes how the $1 million in the revocable trust will be distributed to his heirs, but the distribution plan for the benefits in the insurance trust is locked in—it may not be changed. When Sam dies, the $1 million in the revocable living trust is included in his taxable estate; the $500,000 in the irrevocable insurance trust is not taxed. Assets in both trusts avoid probate.

Gift taxes: Unless the trust has other assets, your continuing payment of the premiums can pose gift tax problems.

Be sure to include the Crummey provision to avoid these taxes.

REVOCABLE INSURANCE TRUSTS

Advantages

Revocability: Flexibility is among the best advantages of revocable trusts. The trust may be changed or canceled anytime during your lifetime. You may add or delete beneficiaries as needed and even change insurance companies and policies.

Probate: Because the trustee is named the beneficiary of the policy, the proceeds avoid probate and are distributed to your beneficiaries immediately after you die, undepleted by lawyers' or court fees.

Income and asset management: The trust lets you determine how and when the insurance proceeds will be paid out.

Disadvantages

Complexity: Creating a separate trust for your insurance means special setup and administration costs. Of course, you can easily avoid these and still get the tax and probate avoidance benefits by naming an existing trust the beneficiary of your insurance policy.

Income: The trust provides you no income from its assets.

Estate taxes: This may be the biggest disadvantage of a revocable insurance trust if your estate is approaching or above the federal exemption ceiling of $600,000. Because you reserve the right to change or cancel the trust at any time, the money is considered part of your taxable estate.

TESTAMENTARY TRUSTS

You may also write your insurance trust into your will. In that event, it will come into existence only after you die. It collects the proceeds of your life insurance policies and holds them in trust for your beneficiaries. Some states allow the proceeds to be released directly to the trustee named in your will without the need for probate—others don't. One reason for creating this kind of trust might be to avoid setting up a trust during your lifetime yet prevent the insurance money from being handed over to your beneficiaries in a lump sum. This trust may be changed anytime before you die simply by changing your will.

CHAPTER 16

CHARITABLE TRUSTS

Many people choose to leave part of their estate to one or more of their favorite charities. Some even leave the bulk of their estate to charity. If you plan to leave a large amount to charities or expect to donate a large amount over the years, it's worth looking into setting up a charitable trust. Depending on the type of charitable trust you create, this can provide you with lifetime income from the assets you plan to donate, reduce the size of your taxable estate and give you a say in how the charity spends your money long after you have died. Before setting up a charitable trust and as you weigh the kinds of charitable trusts described in this chapter, keep in mind the following general considerations.

TAX CUTTING

For many people, the main attraction of a charitable trust is that it lets you give money to the charity of your choice rather than to the IRS. Although any gift to a charitable organization—whether in a will, in a trust or as an outright gift—is exempt from federal income, estate and gift taxes, a charitable trust can allow you to receive income from your assets or assign that income to your family when you die while still receiving tax advantages (see "Income Tax Advantages" later in this chapter).

Although the possible tax benefits are considerable, the tax considerations in setting up a charitable trust can be fairly complex. To ensure that you get the maximum tax advantages, it's advisable to ask a professional to help you set up the trust. You might start by asking the charitable organization you want to name as the trust's beneficiary; many charities have staff that can help you set up your trust so it accommodates both your needs and the organization's and avoids later complications.

A PERPETUAL SAY

You can set up a charitable trust that lasts indefinitely. This is because the public policy that limits the life of all other kinds of trusts and prevents you from controlling your family's spending for generations (see "Rule Against Perpetuities" in Chapter 4) doesn't apply to charitable trusts. Thus, you might establish a charitable trust that endows a permanent chair at a university and, through the instructions you write into the trust document, have some say about how the money is managed and spent indefinitely into the future.

WHAT CHARITIES QUALIFY?

Before setting up a charitable trust, make sure the organization you want to help qualifies as a charity. If it doesn't, you will not get a tax deduction for your donation.

Qualifying charities are those the IRS has determined meet the requirements of tax-exempt nonprofit organizations as spelled out in the IRS code's section 501(c)(3). Most nonprofit organizations—such as the American Cancer Society, your church, your alma mater—qualify as tax-exempt charities; gifts to them will be tax deductible. For-profit entities, on the other hand—even those that do good works, such as private hospitals or clubs, as well as all nonprofit political organizations, such as political parties and political action committees (PACs)—do *not* qualify as charities for tax purposes. You'll get no tax break creating a charitable trust for one of these.

(Incidentally, you should also make sure the charity is willing to be the beneficiary of your gift. Believe it or not, some charities have policies that forbid them to accept certain gifts or prohibit gifts with the strings you may want to attach. For instance, you may want to require that your gift be used to further a program the organization plans to discontinue, or to advocate a policy it has decided not to pursue. The organization will also know what it may and may not do under the law: For example, an organization could jeopardize its tax-exempt status if it participates in political activities, so it may not want gifts that require such activity.)

TRUSTEES

You may name yourself as trustee of your charitable trust, or you may appoint another individual or a bank. Some charities insist on being named trustee so they can use their own expertise in managing the assets; one advantage of this arrangement is that such organizations usually pay the administrative and legal costs of setting up the trust.

WHAT KIND OF TRUST?

Charitable trusts must be irrevocable; you cannot get their tax advantages—usually the prime purpose for creating them—if they're revocable.

Charitable trusts, however, may be either living trusts (created during your lifetime) or testamentary trusts (created in your will). Both kinds lower your federal estate taxes because any charitable gift, whether given before or after you die, is not considered part of your taxable estate. However, to get the full federal income tax advantage during your lifetime, the charitable trust must be both living and irrevocable. You must create it while you're living—not in your will—and you may not change or cancel it at any time: it has to be locked in. Further, to get the deduction, either the trust must pay its income to the charity while you're alive or the income must accumulate in the trust and be turned over to the charity when you die (see "Charitable Lead Trusts" below).

The greatest tax advantages of creating a charitable trust occur if you are in a high income tax bracket and can fund a trust using assets that have appreciated in value since you purchased them—such as a home or stocks—or fund the trust with assets that will continue to produce income. You may not fund your charitable trust with assets you're still paying for, such as a mortgaged home, because they're not yet yours to give away.

INCOME TAX ADVANTAGES

You get an income tax deduction whenever you put anything of value into a charitable trust. No other trust gives you that advantage. This is because funding the trust—putting assets into it—amounts to making a donation to a charitable organization: The donation is deductible from your taxable income with certain limitations, discussed below. Once assets are used to fund an irrevocable charitable trust, they are considered donated for income tax purposes. You may deduct them from your taxable income in the year you transferred them to the trust.

You can get especially big savings if you fund the trust with property that has increased in value significantly since you bought it, because you won't have to pay the taxes you would otherwise owe on the increased value. Ordinarily, if you sell or transfer property to a trust you must pay income taxes on the amount the property is worth at the time of the sale or transfer, minus what it was worth when you acquired it. Giving property that has appreciated in value to a charitable trust is different: In effect, you're giving to charity the profit you would have made had you sold the property, so it's tax free.

Calculating whether it's worth donating property that has increased in value can be complex. Your income tax deduction is usually the current fair market value of the property (what you could get selling it in its current condition), not the value of the property when you acquired it. However, IRS rules differ for various kinds of investments. So before creating a charitable trust, check the rules with someone who knows them (for example, an accountant or tax lawyer) and ask how they'll affect your trust and tax liability.

The amount of charitable donations you may deduct is limited, although that limit is fairly high: up to half of your adjusted gross income, except certain appreciated property, which is limited to 20 percent. Even these limits are offset somewhat, however. Any donation that exceeds the amount you can deduct in one year can be deducted in following years, for up to five years. So even if you fund a charitable trust with proceeds exceeding your one-year limit, you can take advantage of the tax break by spreading your donation across five years.

Finally, if you fund a charitable trust with income-producing property, neither you, the trust nor the charitable organization will have to pay taxes on that income, assuming the trust meets requirements and you don't collect the income yourself. The charitable trust does not itself pay federal income tax on its own income if it is irrevocable and its benefits are assigned only to charity. If the trust was written to allow it, you may change which charities will benefit, but you may not reserve the right to change your mind and leave the trust assets to your family and you may not leave to charity only part of the trust assest—for example, only half of the value of a portfolio of stocks you instruct the trust to sell at your death.

Although the tax advantages are considerable, some people prefer not to set up an irrevocable charitable trust because it means giving up property. Because of this, many choose a middle ground—setting up a charitable trust that names themselves or their families as partial beneficiaries. Such trusts come in three varieties: *charitable remainder trusts, pooled-income funds* and *charitable lead trusts.*

CHARITABLE REMAINDER TRUSTS

Charitable remainder trusts are the most popular of the three because they allow you, or anyone else you name, to receive income from the trust assets until you or your income beneficiary dies, or some other triggering date or event occurs, and then donate the remaining assets—free of estate and gift taxes—to a charity. These trusts give you lifetime income tax advantages and lower the value of your taxable estate when you die. Here's how they work:

• You transfer assets to the trust, naming one or more charities as beneficiaries. The best assets to turn over to the trust, as far as tax advantages are concerned, are those that have grown in value since you bought them, say a piece of property or stocks you bought 10 years ago.
• The trustee—usually you, but you may prefer to name another person, a bank, even the charity you're naming as beneficiary—manages the assets to get the best income possible. The trustee might sell the trust property and invest the proceeds in stocks, certificates of deposit, mutual funds, even other property.

- You instruct the trust to pay you a specified income as long as you live. Your gift is deductible for income tax purposes, but you must subtract the value of the income you will receive. IRS tax valuation forms will tell you how to calculate the amount of your deduction.
- When you or your beneficiary dies, the remainder of the trust assets go to the charity you've named in the document, free of federal estate taxes and probate.

Unitrusts and Annuity Remainder Trusts

Charitable remainder trusts can be of two types: charitable remainder unitrusts and charitable remainder annuity trusts.

Under a *unitrust,* the annual income you receive from the trust fluctuates from year to year, depending on how well the investments perform, but the annual income must normally be at least 5 percent of the fair market value of the trust's assets valued annually. If the trustee's investments do well enough, the available annual income will rise steadily. After you die, what's left in the trust goes to the charity or charities you've selected.

EXAMPLE

Kyle, who is 75, wants to lower his estate tax bill. He decides to donate part of his assets to the American Cancer Society when he dies but wants to continue receiving income from those assets for life. He creates a charitable remainder unitrust and funds it with $100,000 in cash. The trust invests the cash in stocks, bonds and other income-producing assets and pays Kyle 5 percent of the assets' current value each year—initially $5,000. Kyle receives a tax deduction of about $75,000—his $100,000 donation minus his retained-income interest, calculated at about $25,000 using IRS tax tables. Any additional income produced from the trust's investments in stocks and bonds is left to accumulate tax free. When Kyle dies, the remaining assets and accumulated income are turned over to the American Cancer Society free of probate and federal estate and gift taxes.

The *annuity trust* provides you a fixed annual income instead of the unitrust's fluctuating income. The annual income must be at least 5 percent of the assets' original value.

Advantages

Both types of charitable remainder trust have several special advantages:

Income taxes: You're allowed an income tax deduction the year you place your assets into the trust. And you don't pay taxes on the amount of income earned each year by the trust's assets. You pay tax only on that portion paid to you.

Also, you don't pay taxes on the profit the trust makes from the sale of an asset, such as your house, stocks or real estate, used to fund the trust. By putting an asset that has appreciated in value into a charitable remainder trust instead of selling it and giving the proceeds to charity, you avoid taxes on the amount of the appreciation.

Income: The trust provides you income for life.

Estate taxes: The trust reduces or can even eliminate federal estate taxes. The value of your contributions is not included in your estate when federal estate taxes are determined. If your taxable estate, after the charitable deduction, is valued at less than $600,000, no federal estate tax will be due.

Disadvantages

Despite their benefits, charitable remainder trusts also have a number of disadvantages:

Irrevocability: You must give up the right to change or cancel the trust.

Assets: Your family gives away 100 percent of the trust's assets when the trust ends and the assets pass on to the charity.

Asset management: Some charities require that they be appointed trustee and manage the assets as they choose— even if you had someone else in mind for the job. This will mean loss of control over the management of your assets.

Probate: If the trust is created in your will (a testamentary trust) the assets will be subject to the delay and expense of probate when you die.

POOLED-INCOME FUNDS

Some charities maintain or would be willing to set up a pooled-income trust to maximize the money you earn on a smaller charitable gift that it will combine with other similar gifts, much the way a mutual investment fund pools small investments. You might want to look into a pooled-income fund trust if you don't have a lot of valuable assets to donate, or if you prefer making small contributions to a charitable organization over several years. As with other charitable remainder trusts, your taxes will be somewhat lowered.

Pooled-income trusts are irrevocable trusts maintained by the charity, which "pools" your contributions with others. The charity invests the funds and divides the income proportionally among the various contributors or those you and they have designated to receive it—your beneficiaries. Once the beneficiaries of the income have died, 100 percent of your assets pass to the charity.

Advantages

Pooled-income funds offer these benefits:

Income: You or your beneficiaries can receive lifetime income from the income earned by the assets you contribute to the pool.

Income taxes: In the initial year, you may deduct from your taxable income a part of the amount you donate. The deduction will lower your income tax liability and is calculated using IRS tables.

Estate taxes: Your federal estate taxes will be reduced because they are not assessed on money given to charities.

Complexity: The charitable organization manages the trust for you and pays the costs of setting it up.

Disadvantages

These trusts also have some disadvantages:

Irrevocability: As with any charitable trust, to gain the tax advantages you must give up the right to change or cancel the trust.

Assets: Your family gives away 100 percent of your contributions when you or your designated income beneficiary dies. The assets have already been donated to charity.

Asset limitations: Donations must be in the form of cash, stocks or taxable bonds. Pooled funds don't accept real estate and other gifts, even if those assets can be turned into cash.

Asset management: You are not allowed to serve as trustee of the fund, which is maintained by the charity.

CHARITABLE LEAD TRUSTS

The charitable lead trust is the opposite of a charitable remainder trust. It provides income to your favorite charity or charities for a specified period and then distributes the assets to other beneficiaries. The purpose of this trust is to give your beneficiaries an income tax deduction for the income earned by the trust assets. It does this because you donate the trust income to charity without surrendering your beneficiaries' future ownership interest in the trust assets themselves. The "value" of the assets is reduced by the charity's income interest in those assets. Charitable lead trusts are typically testamentary trusts and are always funded with income-producing assets. The IRS has made these trusts less attractive in recent years, so if the idea of establishing one interests you, be sure to talk to an estate specialist.

Advantages

Charitable lead trusts have advantages somewhat different from those of their charitable remainder counterparts.

Income taxes: Your beneficiaries' income taxes are reduced, because the annual income generated by the trust goes to charity.

Assets: At the end of the specified period, 100 percent of the trust's remaining assets passes to your designated heirs.

Disadvantages

The lead trust has these disadvantages:

Irrevocability: You're locked in. You must give up the right to change or cancel the trust.

Income taxes: You get no income tax deduction or shelter when you create this kind of trust because the trust's assets go to other beneficiaries when you die, not to the charity.

Estate taxes: Although the value of the charity's income interest (derived from IRS valuation tables) will reduce the amount of your estate taxes, your estate will have to pay whatever federal estate tax is due on the assets you put into a charitable lead trust.

CHAPTER 17

MISCELLANEOUS TRUSTS

This chapter describes five other types of trusts: *Medicaid qualifying, special-needs, standby, power-of-appointment* and *Totten.* The Medicaid qualifying trust allows you to apply for Medicaid without depleting all your personal assets first. A special-needs trust can improve the standard of living for a disabled child or adult without jeopardizing his or her right to Supplemental Security Income (SSI). The standby trust is used primarily to protect assets if you become seriously ill, the power-of-appointment trust allows you to give someone else the right to distribute your property, and the Totten trust allows money in your bank account to pass on to your beneficiary immediately without having to go through probate.

MEDICAID QUALIFYING TRUSTS

If you (or your spouse) are destined for nursing home care (or think you may be someday because of a degenerative disease like Parkinson's) and are worried about footing the bill—your concerns are understandable. In 1990 Americans spent $53.1 billion on nursing home care, with individual costs running as high as $4,000 to $5,000 a month. If, like most Americans, you haven't planned for long-term care, your life savings, the family home and other personal assets can quickly dissolve into payments for your nursing home care.

This section explains how you can qualify for Medicaid (a government program that picks up, among other things, the cost of long-term nursing home care) without exhausting all of your family's assets first. The catch—and it's a big one—is that you must give up control over your assets by transferring them to another individual (a spouse or child, for example) or by placing them into an irrevocable living trust, such as a Medicaid qualifying trust (MQT). And you must follow strict guidelines for transferring your assets or you may jeopardize your eligibility for Medicaid.

You should also know that because Medicaid is designed for low- to moderately low-income people, the nursing home services provided might not be as good as the services you could have if you purchased them yourself. For example, you may have to share a room and you may not be eligible for as many rehabilitative and recreational activities as you'd like.

Before you irrevocably transfer assets or agree to sacrifices you don't really want to make only to gain Medicaid coverage, you should consult with an estate-planning professional—*someone who is familiar with Medicaid laws.*

Under current Medicaid laws, there are a number of personal assets that are not counted when determining your eligibility. Although Medicaid eligibility requirements vary from state to state (Medicaid is a combined federal and state government program that allows each state to decide its own eligibility requirements within federal guidelines), states typically allow a Medicaid recipient to keep a house, one car, a burial fund, about $2,000 in personal belongings and another $2,000 in personal assets (i.e., cash, stocks or bonds).

If you own a lot more than what Medicaid allows you to keep, you must decide what the safest options are for ridding yourself of excess assets without jeopardizing your eligibility or placing yourself in too precarious a financial situation.

One possible option is the *Medicaid qualifying trust.* A Medicaid qualifying trust is an *irrevocable* living trust that allows you to qualify for Medicaid and, at the same time, protects your assets from claims by the government in connection with the cost of your nursing home care.

For an MQT to work, you must transfer your assets over to the trust at least two and a half years (30 months) before applying for Medicaid benefits. You must give up all rights to the trust principal, and that principal must ultimately be distributed to someone other than you, if you should leave the nursing home, or your estate, when you die. In other words, you can give the principal to your heirs, but not to yourself.

EXAMPLE

Mary Catherine has $200,000 in savings that yields 6 percent interest a year. She puts all of her savings into an irrevocable living trust and directs Dolores, her trustee, to disburse to her the $12,000 in income it produces each year, in quarterly amounts. She sets up the trust so that Dolores has no discretionary power over the trust's principal, only over its income. When Mary Catherine later applies for Medicaid and enters a nursing home four years later, the $12,000 in income goes to help pay the $25,000 annual nursing home bill. Because her $200,000 is inaccessible, Medicaid picks up the rest of the cost. When Mary Catherine dies, her brother Mark will inherit the principal.

Before 1986, a trustee of an MQT was allowed to distribute income and invade the principal on behalf of the grantor without jeopardizing his or her eligibility rights to Medicaid. It was reasoned, in a long line of cases, that because the grantor/beneficiary couldn't demand income or principal from the trust, the trust's assets were not really available to the grantor and were therefore irrelevant to determining Medicaid eligibility, unless, of course, the grantor actually received trust assets. The common practice was to make sure the grantor received no more money than was required to maintain Medicaid eligibility.

Things have changed. Congress passed a law stating that the maximum amount of money that could possibly be paid to the grantor under the terms of the trust, whether or not the money was actually paid, should count as an available asset to the grantor and therefore affect the grantor's Medicaid eligibility. So to ensure Medicaid eligibility under these trusts, you need to severely restrict, if not altogether eliminate, your trustee's discretionary powers.

If your trustee pays you, from the trust's income, more than the amount required for eligibility, the government will deny you coverage because you're making more than the eligibility requirements they set. The government may not invade the trust's principal, however, since neither you nor the trustee has a right to touch it. The laws in this area are still evolving, so be sure to consult someone who is knowledgeable about the latest legal changes.

Also, consider whether you:

- Feel comfortable giving up control over the majority of your assets to qualify for Medicaid coverage
- Will be able to afford housing on the trust's annual income alone if you become well enough to leave the nursing home
- Will be provided for by the people you ultimately give your property to, if it becomes necessary
- Find it ethical, if you can afford to pay for nursing home costs, to shelter your assets and receive public benefits

SPECIAL-NEEDS TRUSTS

Being responsible for the financial security, care and comfort of a disabled child is a challenge most parents want to meet not only during their life but long after they die. Yet leaving money directly to a child who receives government benefits, such as Supplemental Security Income (SSI) will, in all likelihood, jeopardize that child's right to receive public funds.

Short of disinheriting a child to ensure eligibility for government benefits, what can parents do? They can set up a special-needs trust. A special-needs trust provides a disabled person, child or adult, with support that is *above and beyond* what that person already receives from state and local government programs or private agencies. The trust typically pays for items that enhance the well-being of the disabled beneficiary, such as trips to see a friend or relative; tickets to a movie, play or concert; doctor appointments for medical or psychiatric care. It's important that the trustee *supplement,* and not duplicate the public assistance provided, however, or the government may be able to seize the trust's funds or deny government benefits.

Special-needs trusts may be either living or testamentary. For instance, during your lifetime, you and your spouse can create a revocable living trust with yourselves as trustee, a relative or friend as successor trustee and your disabled child as beneficiary. Or you can create a testamentary trust in your will that appoints a relative or other trusted individual to look after your child's needs once you're gone.

To ensure that your child's government benefits are preserved, your trust should include specific language stating its purpose. For example: "to provide benefits or luxuries above and beyond what (your child) receives as a result of his (or her) disability from any local, state or federal government, or from any other private agency."

Your trust should also include language that makes it clear that discretionary power over the trust's funds lies solely with the trustee and that under no circumstances does your disabled child have the right to demand either principal or income.

EXAMPLE

Peter and Lisa set up a revocable living trust to improve the quality of life of their daughter Rebecca. Because of a car accident that left Rebecca partially brain-damaged, she is unable to manage a full-time job but can work part time as a stock clerk in a local grocery store. Her parents wish to supplement Rebecca's part-time income and SSI assistance with money they had planned to leave her after their death. Not wanting to jeopardize her government benefits, they fund a special-needs trust with Rebecca's inheritance and appoint themselves as trustees. They explain to Rebecca that the money is hers to do with as she wants, but to protect her government benefits, they will not distribute funds directly to her but instead will make the expenditures on her behalf. Peter and Lisa also appoint Rebecca's brothers, Philip and Thomas, as successor trustees to manage the trust after they die.

STANDBY TRUSTS

If you want some of the benefits a trust can bring—for example, probate avoidance or management of your assets if you become incapacitated—but do *not* want the expense and trouble of transferring your assets to a trust, you can set up a standby trust. This is an unfunded revocable living trust that doesn't take effect until you die or become physically or mentally incapable of handling your financial affairs. Only at the point of your death or incapacitating illness are your assets transferred to your trust to be managed by the trustee you've selected. Until then, you manage your own assets. They are simply on "standby" for your trust should something happen that renders you incapable of continuing to manage them yourself.

This is how a typical standby trust works:

As grantor, you create and sign a revocable living trust, a durable power of attorney and a pour-over will (see Chapters 9 and 11). You then turn over to your designated trustee the trust, the pour-over will, the power of attorney and all ownership documents for your property. The trustee keeps these documents but does nothing with them until an agreed-upon triggering event—for example, a doctor's ruling that you are incapacitated by Parkinson's disease. (All standby trusts include a provision that specifies who—preferably two doctors you name or allow your trustee or beneficiaries to name—may determine if you are disabled or incompetent.) Only at that point is your trustee authorized by the durable power of attorney to transfer your assets to your trust by retitling all of your ownership documents in the name of the trust. Your trustee then manages your assets until you die (or after your death, if you want) or until you become well enough to take back control of your assets from the trust.

EXAMPLE

Liz, 75, recently had a heart attack and worries that she will have extended periods when she won't be able to manage her finances. She drafts a standby trust that will be activated only if and when she becomes mentally or physically disabled. She names Drs. Richard Brenz and Randy Bramer, who have treated her for 20 years, as the only ones authorized to determine whether she is disabled. Liz allows her niece Rachel to serve as her trustee and to name a backup doctor if Liz's doctors are, for any reason, unavailable. Upon the doctors' determination, Rachel will transfer Liz's assets into the trust and manage them until her aunt dies or her doctor determines she is well enough to manage the assets again. If Liz's assets remain in the trust until she dies, they won't have to go through probate. If she becomes well enough to assume control of them again, then dies while her assets are outside the trust, her estate will have to be probated.

By appointing someone to take over if you become ill or disabled, you accomplish one of the major purposes of a standby trust: eliminating the need for courtroom guardianship proceedings.

These proceedings are required by law before anyone can be declared incompetent to handle her or his own financial affairs. In effect, you replace the legal proceedings with one of your own design.

Another way to avoid the expense and embarrassment guardianship hearings can cause is with a durable power of attorney. This is a legal document that gives someone else the authority to make medical and financial decisions for you if you become ill. However, a durable power of attorney doesn't have the practical value that a standby trust can (but doesn't necessarily) have. Because the power of attorney ends at the death of the person who creates it, it cannot protect that person's estate from probate, nor can the person who is given the power of attorney distribute the property of the deceased person. Instead, another document is needed, such as a will or a trust.

A standby trust might take care of that. Unfortunately, it won't necessarily do so. In fact, it will do so only if your fears are realized and you do become incapacitated. Here's why: If the event that places your assets in the standby trust is your death (say, for example, the incapacity you fear doesn't come to pass and instead you die in your sleep), your assets will have to be probated before being placed into the trust. They were yours, not the trust's, at the moment you died.

To avoid this possibility, if your standby trust is funded with your assets because of your illness and you later become well again, do *not* reclaim the assets from the trust. Leave them where they are and name yourself the trustee. If you choose, you can now name the original trustee your successor, to take over when you die. The assets will then remain in the trust, and at your death the successor trustee will be able to distribute them to your beneficiaries without the hassle or expense of going through probate. Of course, this works only if you do become incapacitated at least once and trigger the trust into action. If the standby trust isn't activated before you die, it can't keep your assets out of probate.

Obviously, the safest way to make sure your property is managed the way you want and avoids probate, regardless of whether you become incapacitated, is to follow the route described in Chapter 9: Fund a revocable living trust from the start, and appoint yourself trustee and someone else as successor trustee to step in when you die or if you become incapacitated. Otherwise, you won't be guaranteed that your estate will avoid probate.

POWER-OF-APPOINTMENT TRUSTS

Although sometimes used in a marital trust (see Chapter 13), other trusts can use a power-of-appointment (POA) clause when you aren't sure who you want to have inherit your assets. This is not a common problem; most people know to whom they want to leave their property. Still, a power of appointment does offer flexibility for those few who are unsure (for example, a childless couple with many relatives) and those waiting to decide on their beneficiaries until future events unfold, such as the birth of grandchildren.

A POA trust may be either a living or testamentary trust. You can create it during your lifetime or write it into your will, to be created at your death.

A POA trust confers on trustees, successor trustees or even income beneficiaries the power to distribute trust property as they see fit after you die. As you might guess, that authority may be granted either broadly or within narrowly defined limits. In fact, two types of powers can be conferred—a *general* power of appointment and a *special* (or *limited*) power of appointment. The difference is important not only for what amount of authority over your property you give away, but also because of the tax implications.

Whomever you give a general power of appointment to in

a trust may give the property to anyone they want, including themselves, their own estate, their creditors or the creditors of their estate. Because they have total control over the assets placed into the trust, federal tax collectors treat them as though they actually own the property: The value of the trust assets is included in *their* taxable estate when they die. Because of this, it is unusual for anyone to grant a general power of appointment other than in a marital trust, as described in Chapter 13.

Giving a special or limited power of appointment is much more common and far less risky. This restricts the recipients' powers by forbidding them to give trust property to themselves, their estates or their creditors. They may, however, give property to anyone not in one of those categories. Because they personally do not have any legal rights to the property, it will not be included in their taxable estate.

You can name a class of persons (such as your children, grandchildren, nieces or nephews) as your beneficiaries and instruct the trustee to award the trust assets to whichever of these is most deserving or needy at the time. Or you might instruct the trustee to use other criteria, for example, distributing the assets to those from your group of potential beneficiaries who attend college, those who undergo medical emergencies or those who face other special needs.

EXAMPLE

Mike and Myrna, a childless couple in their 80s, have 20 grand-nieces and grandnephews, but they don't know how needy each child is and they do not want to burden themselves with trying to find out. Their solution is to create a special power-of-appointment trust that will take effect when they die. Mike's youngest sister's daughter, Andrea, will be trustee. In the trust, Mike and Myrna instruct Andrea to distribute the trust income and assets to their grandnieces and grandnephews according to need until the youngest reaches age 30, at which time all remaining assets are to be divided equally among all 20. Because they wrote the trust into their will and it won't receive their assets until after both Mike and Myrna have died, their assets will have to be probated.

As you might expect, setting up a power-of-appointment trust is not common. It can, however, be created in combination with any of several types of trust discussed in this book. Its purpose has to do with the powers assigned the trustee, not with whether the trust is revocable or irrevocable or living or testamentary. Mike and Myrna, in the example above, weren't required to write it into their will. Instead, they might have created it as a living trust and thereby kept the assets out of probate.

The POA trust can be written as part of a trust that's created between spouses to distribute their property after both die (Chapter 13), or as a special trust set up for children (Chapter 14).

If you're interested in creating a POA trust, you probably should consult an estate-planning professional.

TOTTEN TRUSTS

Totten trusts (also called *bank account* or *pay-on-death account* trusts) usually are created by people who have modest estates and who intend to dispose of their property in a will but may want to take advantage of a few probate-avoidance tools. These trusts are not typically used by people with large or complicated estates.

Totten trusts are revocable living trusts that allow you to place your bank account money into a trust for someone else. Because your account is revocable, you maintain complete control over your money: You can make as many deposits and withdrawals as you want, change or add beneficiaries or even close out the account. Your Totten trust beneficiaries inherit what's left in the account after you die, without having to go through probate. They never have a legal claim to the account while you're alive, however.

As discussed in Chapter 3, you could achieve part of that objective by setting up a joint bank account instead. That would give your beneficiary immediate, probate-free access to your money after you die. Of course, it also gives the joint account owner equal rights to whatever money is in the account while you're alive. And if the joint owner ever applies for public benefits, such as Medicaid or SSI, the entire amount will be deemed available to him or her and could affect his or her eligibility. If these issues are of concern, you probably should consider a Totten trust.

Creating one is easy. Most banking institutions will do the paperwork without charge. You'll get the account ownership document—a passbook, savings statement or certificate of deposit (CD)—that bears both your name and the name of your beneficiary. The document might identify the account as owned by "David Worden, Trustee for Julia Worden, Beneficiary." The words "Totten trust" might not appear on the document, but that is what it is.

Because banks use different names for Totten trusts and because some banks use them more often than others, you may run into a blank stare if you use the term. Don't be put off. Simply explain that you want to put your bank account into trust for someone else; almost any bank employee qualified to open an account should be able to help. Before signing any document, however, be sure to ask about the rules governing these trusts in your state. Some states require that you notify your beneficiaries before you set up a Totten trust, and in most states your spouse has a right to a share of the account regardless of whom you name as beneficiary.

When you die, all your beneficiary has to do to collect the money is present the bank with proof of identity (such as a driver's license or student ID) and a certified copy of your death certificate. The money collected will not go through probate. If the beneficiary is a minor, a legal guardian will have to present the bank with the appropriate papers instead.

One final warning: Money in a Totten trust account is covered by FDIC insurance only if your beneficiary is a spouse, child or grandchild. Totten trusts for other relatives and for nonrelatives are not insured by the FDIC.

Conclusion

Trusts are highly flexible tools. In fact, you can design a trust to achieve almost any estate-planning goal you can imagine—as long as it's legal. And in many cases you can also get some substantial tax breaks and probate-avoidance savings.

Ultimately, whether you should use a trust depends on you: your assessment of your own needs and goals and your willingness to figure out your options.

If you decide you can benefit from a trust and think you know which kind you want to create, explore your options for drafting it. Each of the chapters on specific kinds of trusts has indicated when seeking professional help may be advisable or essential. Before setting out to create a trust, however, we suggest you review Chapter 8.

Trusts and the rules that govern them are constantly changing, the options expanding and contracting with each change in tax and probate laws. Each year, new kinds of trusts attempt to exploit newly discovered loopholes in tax laws and new tax laws are written to close those loopholes.

Although this creates some confusion for anyone trying to stay abreast of the laws that govern trusts, the situation isn't as bleak as in many other areas of the law. Bookstores are well stocked with titles explaining the latest in trusts, many of the books in plain language. It is our hope that this book has proved a valuable addition to the plain-language library on trusts and that it answers all but your most technical questions in straightforward language. Our bibliography (Appendix VII) includes many other books, making up a cross section of the popular literature that's currently available.

Reforms that standardize and streamline requirements might someday make trusts even more accessible and convenient to nonlawyers. Technological advances will certainly have an impact, providing more and more computerized programs and forms. Whatever lies in the future, trusts are one corner of the legal arena in which individuals can and already do exercise a significant degree of autonomy over their personal affairs. By reading this book and considering whether trusts might play a valuable role in your estate plan and then by undertaking to prepare your own trust—whether by yourself or with professional help—you are already participating in and adding to that autonomy.

STATE RULES

This appendix lists the statutory laws regulating trusts for all 50 states, the District of Columbia, Puerto Rico and the Virgin Islands. As noted in Chapter 4, however, the laws governing trusts are created more often in court, on a case-by-case basis, than in state legislatures. If you plan to research trust laws for your state, you should consult both case and statute law.

Researching statutes for information about trusts is not difficult but may take extra time since the laws governing trusts are not always found in the same volume of your state's statutes. For example, the answer to a question about *whether a trust must be in writing* is usually found in statutes dealing with contracts, which may or may not be in the same volume as that discussing trust laws.

The following notes should help you understand the entries in this appendix. You can also check the glossary for any terms in italics. Categories and headings not discussed in this section are self-explanatory.

Uniform Acts Adopted

The following acts have been adopted in full by many states. This appendix indicates whether your state has adopted one or more of these acts.

The *Uniform Probate Code* includes provisions that simplify the probate process by minimizing the amount of reporting and court supervision time needed to probate a will or testamentary trust. While the code concentrates on probate procedures, it also includes provisions relating to trusts and trustees; for example, what trustees may charge, whether they have to post bond (buy insurance coverage to compensate you if they should steal your trust funds) and so on.

The *Uniform Trustees' Powers Act* outlines what a trustee may and may not do. This act is typically referred to when a trustee's powers are not spelled out in the trust document or when there is a dispute over the powers that are spelled out. It describes approximately 30 different types of powers that a trustee may employ, including the power to buy, invest and sell trust property.

The *Uniform Testamentary Additions to Trusts Act* allows property to be transferred from a person's will to his or her living trust after he or she dies. For that to happen, however, the person setting up the living trust has to draft a separate document known as a pour-over will (see Chapter 11) and include in it a specific pour-over provision. The few states that have not adopted this act have adopted similar pour-over statutes.

The *Uniform Statutory Rule Against Perpetuities* is explained below under "Rule Against Perpetuities." It has been adopted by 16 states and is pending in another three (Alaska, New Mexico and West Virginia).

Must Trustee Be a State Resident?

Every state allows you to appoint an out-of-state trustee to your trust but may require that trustee to do one of several things. Some states require nonresident trustees to register the trust (if it's testamentary) with the probate court in the county where the grantor lived. Others require a *resident agent* (someone who lives in state and can accept legal documents) to be appointed. Or a state may require an out-of-state trustee to register to do business in the state.

Registering is typically done at the probate court or at the secretary of state's office.

May Creditors Reach Beneficiary's Income?

Creditors in every state may reach a beneficiary's trust income to satisfy a debt. However, if a *spendthrift* provision has been included in a trust, a creditor's right to the beneficiary's income is severely restricted. It varies with each state, but typically a beneficiary's income can be reached when only it is due and payable to the beneficiary or when the beneficiary owes money for alimony, child support payments, taxes or necessities provided to them (for example, medical care or tuition costs).

Must the Trust Be in Writing?

All states require trusts including real estate to be in writing. Trusts holding personal property may usually be written or oral. As we suggest in Chapter 4, however, it's always a good idea to put your trust into writing to prevent any misunderstanding about your intentions.

Rule Against Perpetuities

This rule governs how long a trust may last. It applies only to private trusts—not charitable trusts. Less than half the states still adhere to the rule against perpetuities in full (known as the common-law rule). Well over half the states have adopted a modified "wait-and-see" version of the common-law rule.

The common-law rule states that a trust may not last longer than the life of a person already alive at the time the trust is created plus an additional 21 years. If the trust might possibly last longer, it is considered illegal or void.

The modified "wait-and-see" version of this rule allows a wait, to see what really happens. If the beneficiary obtains a full interest in the trust property within the time limits of the rule, the trust is deemed valid even if it's possible that the beneficiary might not have obtained a full interest in time. Nearly all trusts turn out to be valid under the wait-and-see rule.

Most of the "wait-and-see" states have adopted the new *Uniform Statutory Rule Against Perpetuities,* which simplifies the process for determining whether a trust violates the rule against perpetuities. It allows a court to modify a trust if, after the wait-and-see period expires, the trust would still be invalid. The court must then modify the trust to make it valid.

Alabama

Uniform acts adopted: Uniform Testamentary Additions to Trusts Act.

Must trustee be a state resident? No provision.

Can creditors reach beneficiary's income? Yes. If spendthrift trust is for blood or marriage relative, trust income cannot be reached by creditors.

Must the trust be in writing? A trust holding real estate must be in writing. A trust holding personal or other property can be written or oral.

Must trustee post bond? No provision.

Pour-over statute: The trust must be identified in the will. The terms of the trust must be in a document other than the will and signed before or at the same time as the will.

Age of majority to be grantor or trustee: 19.

Rule against perpetuities: The common-law rule applies.

Forms of property ownership: Common-law state. Tenancy in common presumed if real estate is held jointly, unless title creates joint tenancy with right of survivorship or similar words. No tenancy in entirety.

Joint bank accounts: Deposits payable to any survivor.

Note: Trusts are considered irrevocable unless powers to revoke are stated.

Alaska

Uniform acts adopted: Uniform Probate Code; Uniform Testamentary Additions to Trusts Act.

Must trustee be a state resident? No, but if out-of-state trustee is appointed, trust must be registered.

Can creditors reach beneficiary's income? No provision.

Must the trust be in writing? Yes, all trusts must be in writing.

Must trustee post bond? No, unless required by trust, requested by beneficiary or ordered by court.

Pour-over statute: The trust must be identified in the will. The terms of the trust must be in a document other than the will and signed before or at the same time as the will.

Age of majority to be grantor or trustee: 18.

Rule against perpetuities: Wait-and-see approach; common-law rule is modified by actual rather than possible events.

Forms of property ownership: Common-law state. No joint tenancy in personal property. Persons with undivided interests in real estate are tenants in common. Spouses who acquire real estate hold it as tenants by entirety unless stated otherwise.

Joint bank accounts: Deposits payable to any survivor.

Arizona

Uniform acts adopted: Uniform Probate Code; Uniform Trustees' Powers Act; Uniform Testamentary Additions to Trusts Act.

Must trustee be a state resident? No, but if out-of-state trustee is appointed, must qualify to do business in Arizona.

Can creditors reach beneficiary's income? Yes. If spendthrift trust, income can be reached when due and payable.

Must the trust be in writing? A trust holding real estate must be in writing. A trust holding personal property can be written or oral.

Must trustee post bond? No, unless required by trust.

Pour-over statute: The trust must be identified in the will. The terms of the trust must be in a document other than the will and signed before or at the same time as the will.

Age of majority to be grantor or trustee: 18.

Rule against perpetuities: The common-law rule applies.

Forms of property ownership: Community property state. Property acquired during marriage outside state before moving into state is quasi–community property controlled by Arizona law. Joint tenancy between spouses if stated. No tenancy by entirety.

Joint bank accounts: Deposits payable to any survivor unless clear and convincing evidence exists that deposit is payable only to specified survivor(s).

Arkansas

Uniform acts adopted: Uniform Testamentary Additions to Trusts Act.

Must trustee be a state resident? No, but if out-of-state trustee is appointed, must qualify to do business in Arkansas.

Can creditors reach beneficiary's income? Yes. If spendthrift trust, income can be reached when due and payable or to satisfy alimony or child support payments.

Must the trust be in writing? A trust holding real estate must be in writing.

Must trustee post bond? Yes, unless not required by trust.

Pour-over statute: The trust must be identified in the will. The terms of the trust must be in a document other than the will and signed before or at the same time as the will.

Age of majority to be grantor or trustee: 18.

Rule against perpetuities: The common-law rule applies.

Forms of property ownership: Common-law state. Property acquired in another state is community property if considered so in other state. Tenancy in common, joint tenancy recognized. Tenancy by entirety recognized when conveyed to husband and wife.

Joint bank accounts: Deposits payable to any survivor.

Note: If all beneficiaries consent, trust can be revoked, modified or terminated.

California

Uniform acts adopted: Uniform Testamentary Additions to Trusts Act; Uniform Statutory Rule Against Perpetuities.

Must trustee be a state resident? No, but if out-of-state trustee is appointed, trustee's actions are severely restricted.

Can creditors reach beneficiary's income? Yes. If spendthrift trust, income can be reached when due and payable, when needed to satisfy alimony or child support payments or when surplus beyond what is needed for education and support of beneficiary exists.

Must the trust be in writing? A trust holding real estate must be in writing.

Must trustee post bond? No, unless required by trust.

Pour-over statute: The trust must be identified in the will. The terms of the trust must be in a document other than the will and signed before or at the same time as the will.

Age of majority to be grantor or trustee: 18.

Rule against perpetuities: The common-law rule is modified by wait-and-see approach.

Forms of property ownership: Community property state.

Property in names of spouses as joint tenants is not community property unless stated. Joint tenancy must be stated. No tenancy by entirety.

Joint bank accounts: Deposits payable to survivor if account had rights of survivorship provision.

Colorado

Uniform acts adopted: Uniform Probate Code; Uniform Testamentary Additions to Trusts Act; Uniform Statutory Rule Against Perpetuities.

Must trustee be a state resident? No, but if out-of-state trustee is appointed, trust must be registered.

Can creditors reach beneficiary's income? Yes. If spendthrift trust, income can be reached when beneficiary is also grantor.

Must the trust be in writing? A trust holding real estate must be in writing.

Must trustee post bond? No, unless required by trust or requested by beneficiary.

Pour-over statute: The trust must be identified in the will. The terms of the trust must be in a document other than the will and signed before or at the same time as the will.

Age of majority to be grantor or trustee: 18.

Rule against perpetuities: The common-law rule is modified by wait-and-see approach.

Forms of property ownership: Common-law state. Tenancy in common presumed unless otherwise stated. Joint tenancy recognized. No tenancy by entirety.

Joint bank accounts: Deposits payable to any survivor.

Connecticut

Uniform acts adopted: Uniform Testamentary Additions to Trusts Act; Uniform Statutory Rule Against Perpetuities.

Must trustee be a state resident? No, but if out-of-state trustee is appointed, a resident agent must also be appointed.

Can creditors reach beneficiary's income? Yes. If spendthrift trust, income can be reached when due and payable as long as it hasn't been given for support of beneficiary.

Must the trust be in writing? A trust holding real estate must be in writing.

Must trustee post bond? Yes, unless not required by trust.

Pour-over statute: The trust must be identified in the will. The

terms of the trust must be in a document other than the will and signed before or at the same time as the will.

Age of majority to be grantor or trustee: 21.

Rule against perpetuities: The common-law rule is modified by wait-and-see approach.

Forms of property ownership: Common-law state. In joint ownership, tenancy in common presumed unless words "joint tenants" follow names. Joint tenancy automatically includes right of survivorship. No tenancy by entirety.

Joint bank accounts: Deposits payable to any survivor.

Delaware

Uniform acts adopted: None.

Must trustee be a state resident? No.

Can creditors reach beneficiary's income? Yes. If spendthrift trust, income cannot be reached unless trust was set up to defraud creditors.

Must the trust be in writing? A trust holding real estate must be in writing.

Must trustee post bond? No provision.

Pour-over statute: The trust must be identified in the will. The terms of the trust must be in a document other than the will and signed before or at the same time as the will.

Age of majority to be grantor or trustee: 18.

Rule against perpetuities: The common-law rule is modified by wait-and-see approach.

Forms of property ownership: Common-law state. Tenancy in common presumed. If joint owners are married, tenancy by entirety created. Joint tenancy created only if stated.

Joint bank accounts: Deposits payable to any survivor.

District of Columbia

Uniform acts adopted: Uniform Testamentary Additions to Trusts Act.

Must trustee be a state resident? No provision.

Can creditors reach beneficiary's income? Yes. No information found on spendthrift trusts.

Must the trust be in writing? A trust holding real estate must be in writing.

Must trustee post bond? Yes, if appointed by court.

Pour-over statute: The trust must be identified in the will. The terms of the trust must be in a document other than the will and signed before or at the same time as the will.

Age of majority to be grantor or trustee: 18.

Rule against perpetuities: The common-law rule applies.

Forms of property ownership: Common-law state. Tenancy in common presumed unless joint tenancy stated. Joint tenancy, tenancy by entirety can be created if at least one of the granting owners is also a recipient owner. Joint ownership by husband and wife presumes tenancy by entirety.

Joint bank accounts: Deposits payable to any survivor.

Florida

Uniform acts adopted: Uniform Trustees' Powers Act; Uniform Testamentary Additions to Trusts Act; Uniform Statutory Rule Against Perpetuities.

Must trustee be a state resident? No, but if out-of-state trustee is appointed, may be required to register trust if requested by beneficiary or directed by trust.

Can creditors reach beneficiary's income? Yes. No information found on spendthrift trusts.

Must the trust be in writing? A trust holding real estate must be in writing.

Must trustee post bond? No, unless required by trust, requested by beneficiary or ordered by court.

Pour-over statute: The trust must be identified in the will. The terms of the trust must be in a document other than the will and signed before or at the same time as the will.

Age of majority to be grantor or trustee: 18.

Rule against perpetuities: The common-law rule is modified by wait-and-see approach.

Forms of property ownership: Common-law state. Personal property or real estate owned by husband and wife presumes tenancy by entirety and survivorship. Joint tenancy includes survivorship only if stated.

Joint bank accounts: Deposits payable to any survivor.

Georgia

Uniform acts adopted: Uniform Testamentary Additions to Trusts Act; Uniform Statutory Rule Against Perpetuities.

Must trustee be a state resident? No.

Can creditors reach beneficiary's income? Yes. If spendthrift trust, income can be reached when due and payable; principal can be reached to satisfy alimony or child support payments or for necessities provided to beneficiary by creditor.

Must the trust be in writing? A trust holding real estate must be in writing.

Must trustee post bond? Court may require a successor trustee to post bond; otherwise, not unless required by trust or requested by beneficiary.

Pour-over statute: The trust must be identified in the will. The terms of the trust must be in a document other than the will and signed before or at the same time as the will.

Age of majority to be grantor or trustee: 18.

Rule against perpetuities: The common-law rule is modified by wait-and-see approach.

Forms of property ownership: Common-law state. Tenancy in common presumed unless ownership papers refer to "joint tenants" or similar language. No tenancy by entirety.

Joint bank accounts: Deposits payable to any survivor unless clear and convincing evidence exists that deposit is payable only to specified survivor(s).

Hawaii

Uniform acts adopted: Uniform Trustees' Powers Act; Uniform Testamentary Additions to Trusts Act.

Must trustee be a state resident? No, but if out-of-state trustee is appointed to a living trust, trust must be registered.

Can creditors reach beneficiary's income? Yes. If spendthrift trust, income can be reached when due and payable; principal can be reached to satisfy alimony or child support payments; principal and income can be reached when trust is set up to defraud creditors.

Must the trust be in writing? A trust holding real estate must be in writing.

Must trustee post bond? No, unless required by trust, requested by beneficiary or ordered by court.

Pour-over statute: The trust must be identified in the will. The terms of the trust must be in a document other than the will and signed before or at the same time as the will.

Age of majority to be grantor or trustee: 18.

Rule against perpetuities: The common-law rule applies.

Forms of property ownership: Common-law state. Tenancy in common presumed unless stated as joint tenancy or tenancy by entirety.

Joint bank accounts: Deposits payable to any survivor unless clear and convincing evidence exists that deposit is payable only to specified survivor(s).

Idaho

Uniform acts adopted: Uniform Probate Code; Uniform Trustees' Powers Act; Uniform Testamentary Additions to Trusts Act.

Must trustee be a state resident? No, but if out-of-state trustee is appointed, must qualify to do business in Idaho. A trustee, whether a resident or not, must register the trust.

Can creditors reach beneficiary's income? Yes. If spendthrift trust, income can be reached when due and payable; principal can be reached to satisfy alimony or child support payments or for necessities provided to beneficiary by creditor.

Must the trust be in writing? A trust holding real estate must be in writing.

Must trustee post bond? No, unless required by trust, requested by beneficiary or ordered by court.

Pour-over statute: The trust must be identified in the will. The terms of the trust must be in a document other than the will and signed before or at the same time as the will.

Age of majority to be grantor or trustee: 18.

Rule against perpetuities: Wait-and-see approach; common-law rule is modified by actual rather than possible events.

Forms of property ownership: Community property state. Tenancy in common presumed unless joint tenancy stated or property is acquired as partnership or community property. Tenancy by entirety not recognized.

Joint bank accounts: Deposits payable to any survivor unless clear and convincing evidence exists that deposit is payable only to specified survivor(s).

Illinois

Uniform acts adopted: Uniform Testamentary Additions to Trusts Act.

Must trustee be a state resident? No.

Can creditors reach beneficiary's income? Yes. If spendthrift trust, income can be reached when due and payable; income and principal can be reached to satisfy alimony or child support payments or for necessities provided to beneficiary by creditor.

Must the trust be in writing? A trust holding real estate must be in writing.

Must trustee post bond? No, unless required by trust.

Pour-over statute: The trust must be identified in the will. The

terms of the trust must be in a document other than the will and signed before or at the same time as the will.

Age of majority to be grantor or trustee: 18.

Rule against perpetuities: Wait-and-see approach; common-law rule is modified by actual rather than possible events.

Forms of property ownership: Common-law state. Tenancy in common presumed. Joint tenancy with right of survivorship created only by declaration that estate, including personal property, is in joint tenancy and not tenancy in common. Tenancy by entirety recognized.

Joint bank accounts: Deposits payable to any survivor.

Indiana

Uniform acts adopted: Uniform Testamentary Additions to Trusts Act; Uniform Statutory Rule Against Perpetuities.

Must trustee be a state resident? No.

Can creditors reach beneficiary's income? Yes. If spendthrift trust, income can be reached when due and payable or to satisfy alimony or child support payments.

Must the trust be in writing? Yes.

Must trustee post bond? No, unless required by trust.

Pour-over statute: The trust must be identified in the will. The terms of the trust must be in a document other than the will and signed before or at the same time as the will.

Age of majority to be grantor or trustee: 18.

Rule against perpetuities: The common-law rule is modified by wait-and-see approach.

Forms of property ownership: Common-law state. Joint tenancy, tenancy in common and tenancy by entirety recognized. For real estate jointly owned (except by married couples), tenancy in common presumed unless joint tenancy stated. Joint ownership by husband and wife presumes tenancy by entirety.

Joint bank accounts: Deposits payable to any survivor.

Iowa

Uniform acts adopted: Uniform Testamentary Additions to Trusts Act.

Must trustee be a state resident? No.

Can creditors reach beneficiary's income? Yes. If spendthrift trust, income can be reached to satisfy alimony or child support payments.

Must the trust be in writing? A trust holding real estate must be in writing.

Must trustee post bond? No, unless required by trust or ordered by court.

Pour-over statute: The trust must be identified in the will. The terms of the trust must be in a document other than the will and signed before or at the same time as the will.

Age of majority to be grantor or trustee: 18.

Rule against perpetuities: Wait-and-see approach; common-law rule modified by actual rather than possible events.

Forms of property ownership: Common-law state. Tenancy in common presumed unless joint tenancy stated. No tenancy by entirety.

Joint bank accounts: Deposits payable to any survivor.

Kansas

Uniform acts adopted: Uniform Trustees' Powers Act; Uniform Testamentary Additions to Trusts Act.

Must trustee be a state resident? No, but if out-of-state trustee is appointed, a resident agent must also be appointed.

Can creditors reach beneficiary's income? Yes. If spendthrift trust, income can be reached when due and payable, principal cannot be reached.

Must the trust be in writing? A trust holding real estate must be in writing.

Must trustee post bond? Yes, unless not required by trust.

Pour-over statute: The trust must be identified in the will. The terms of the trust must be in a document other than the will and signed before or at the same time as the will.

Age of majority to be grantor or trustee: 18.

Rule against perpetuities: The common-law rule applies, although a trust holding a stock bonus plan, pension plan, disability or death-benefit plan is exempt from the rule against perpetuities.

Forms of property ownership: Common-law state. Tenancy in common presumed unless joint tenancy stated and transfer is from sole owner to himself or herself and one other. No tenancy by entirety.

Joint bank accounts: Deposits payable to any survivor.

Kentucky

Uniform acts adopted: Uniform Trustees' Powers Act; Uniform Testamentary Additions to Trusts Act.

Must trustee be a state resident? No provision.

Can creditors reach beneficiary's income? Yes. If spendthrift trust, income can be reached to satisfy alimony or child support payments, for taxes or for necessities provided to beneficiary by creditor. Income can also be reached if beneficiary is grantor.

Must the trust be in writing? A trust holding real estate must be in writing.

Must trustee post bond? No, unless required by trust, requested by beneficiary or ordered by court.

Pour-over statute: The trust must be identified in the will. The terms of the trust must be in a document other than the will and signed before or at the same time as the will.

Age of majority to be grantor or trustee: 18.

Rule against perpetuities: Wait-and-see approach; common-law rule is modified by actual rather than possible events.

Forms of property ownership: Common-law state. Tenancy in common presumed between husband and wife unless joint tenancy stated. Tenancy by entirety recognized.

Joint bank accounts: Deposits payable to any survivor.

Louisiana

Uniform acts adopted: None.

Must trustee be a state resident? No.

Can creditors reach beneficiary's income? Yes. If spendthrift trust, income and principal can be reached if beneficiary is grantor, to satisfy alimony or child support payments, to pay for necessaries provided to beneficiary by creditor or for an offense committed by beneficiary who is individually responsible.

Must the trust be in writing? A trust holding real estate must be in writing.

Must trustee post bond? Yes, unless not required by trust.

Pour-over statute: The trust must be identified in the will. The terms of the trust must be in a document other than the will and signed before or at the same time as the will.

Age of majority to be grantor or trustee: 18.

Rule against perpetuities: The common-law rule applies.

Forms of property ownership: Community property state. Joint ownership (called indivision) if two or more persons listed as owners. No tenancy by entirety or tenancy in common.

Joint bank accounts: Deposits payable to any survivor.

Note: Every donation made to a spouse is considered irrevocable unless the power to revoke trust is stated.

Maine

Uniform acts adopted: Uniform Probate Code; Uniform Testamentary Additions to Trusts Act.

Must trustee be a state resident? No, but if out-of-state trustee is appointed, must qualify to do business in Maine.

Can creditors reach beneficiary's income? Yes. If spendthrift trust, income can be reached when due and payable but trustee can withhold that amount.

Must the trust be in writing? A trust holding real estate must be in writing.

Must trustee post bond? No, unless required by trust, requested by beneficiary or ordered by court.

Pour-over statute: The trust must be identified in the will. The terms of the trust must be in a document other than the will and signed before or at the same time as the will.

Age of majority to be grantor or trustee: 18.

Rule against perpetuities: The common-law rule applies.

Forms of property ownership: Common-law state. Ownership by two or more presumes tenancy in common unless joint tenancy stated. No tenancy by entirety.

Joint bank accounts: Deposits payable to any survivor.

Maryland

Uniform acts adopted: Uniform Testamentary Additions to Trusts Act.

Must trustee be a state resident? No provision.

Can creditors reach beneficiary's income? Yes. No information found on spendthrift trusts.

Must the trust be in writing? A trust holding real estate must be in writing.

Must trustee post bond? No.

Pour-over statute: The trust must be identified in the will. The terms of the trust must be in a document other than the will and signed before or at the same time as the will.

Age of majority to be grantor or trustee: 18.

Rule against perpetuities: The common-law rule applies.

Forms of property ownership: Common-law state. Tenancy in common recognized. Joint tenancy must be stated. Joint ownership by spouses presumes tenancy by entirety unless stated otherwise.

Joint bank accounts: Deposits payable to any survivor.

Massachusetts

Uniform acts adopted: Uniform Testamentary Additions to Trusts Act; Uniform Statutory Rule Against Perpetuities.

Must trustee be a state resident? No, but if out-of-state trustee is appointed and trust holds Massachusetts land, trust must be registered.

Can creditors reach beneficiary's income? Yes. No information found on spendthrift trusts.

Must the trust be in writing? A trust holding real estate must be in writing.

Must trustee post bond? No, unless required by trust.

Pour-over statute: The trust must be identified in the will. The terms of the trust must be in a document other than the will and signed before or at the same time as the will.

Age of majority to be grantor or trustee: 18.

Rule against perpetuities: The common-law rule is modified by wait-and-see approach.

Forms of property ownership: Common-law state. Tenancy in common, joint tenancy and tenancy by entirety recognized. Joint ownership by husband and wife creates tenancy in common, unless otherwise stated.

Joint bank accounts: Deposits payable to any survivor.

Michigan

Uniform acts adopted: Uniform Probate Code; Uniform Testamentary Additions to Trusts Act; Uniform Statutory Rule Against Perpetuities.

Must trustee be a state resident? No, but if out-of-state trustee is appointed, must qualify to do business in Michigan.

Can creditors reach beneficiary's income? Yes. If spendthrift trust, income can be reached to satisfy alimony and child support payments. Also, surplus income beyond what is needed for education and support of beneficiary can be reached.

Must the trust be in writing? Yes.

Must trustee post bond? No, unless required by trust.

Pour-over statute: The trust must be identified in the will. The terms of the trust must be in a document other than the will and signed before or at the same time as the will.

Age of majority to be grantor or trustee: 18.

Rule against perpetuities: The common-law rule is modified by wait-and-see approach.

Forms of property ownership: Common-law state. Tenancy in common, joint tenancy and tenancy by entirety recognized. Joint tenancy created only if stated. Joint tenancy by spouses and joint ownership of real estate by spouses presumed tenancy by entirety unless otherwise stated. Joint tenancy with right of survivorship recognized for bank accounts, securities, safe deposit box contents, but intent must be in writing.

Joint bank accounts: Deposits payable to any survivor.

Minnesota

Uniform acts adopted: Uniform Probate Code; Uniform Trustees' Powers Act; Uniform Testamentary Additions to Trusts Act; Uniform Statutory Rule Against Perpetuities.

Must trustee be a state resident? No provision.

Can creditors reach beneficiary's income? Yes. If spendthrift trust, income cannot be reached by creditors.

Must the trust be in writing? Yes.

Must trustee post bond? No provision.

Pour-over statute: The trust must be identified in the will. The terms of the trust must be in a document other than the will and signed before or at the same time as the will.

Age of majority to be grantor or trustee: 18.

Rule against perpetuities: The common-law rule is modified by wait-and-see approach.

Forms of property ownership: Common-law state. Tenancy in common presumed unless joint tenancy in writing. No tenancy by entirety.

Joint bank accounts: Deposits payable to any survivor unless clear and convincing evidence exists that deposit is payable only to specified survivor(s).

Mississippi

Uniform acts adopted: Uniform Trustees' Powers Act; Uniform Testamentary Additions to Trusts Act.

Must trustee be a state resident? No, but if out-of-state trustee is appointed, must qualify to do business in Mississippi.

Can creditors reach beneficiary's income? Yes. No information found on spendthrift trusts.

Must the trust be in writing? Yes.

Must trustee post bond? No, unless required by trust.

Pour-over statute: The trust must be identified in the will. The terms of the trust must be in a document other than the will and signed before or at the same time as the will.

Age of majority to be grantor or trustee: 18.

Rule against perpetuities: The common-law rule applies.

Forms of property ownership: Common-law state. Tenancy in common, joint tenancy and tenancy by entirety recognized. Ownership by two or more persons presumes tenancy in common unless joint tenancy stated.

Joint bank accounts: Deposits payable to any survivor.

Note: Trusts can be modified even when power to revoke is not stated.

Missouri

Uniform acts adopted: None.

Must trustee be a state resident? No, but if out-of-state trustee is appointed, must qualify to do business in Missouri.

Can creditors reach beneficiary's income? Yes. If spendthrift trust, income can be reached to satisfy alimony or child support payments, for necessities provided to beneficiary by creditor, if trust was set up to defraud creditors, if sole beneficiary of a revocable trust is also grantor or if grantor was one of a class of beneficiaries and retained a right to a specific portion of income and principal.

Must the trust be in writing? A trust holding real estate must be in writing.

Must trustee post bond? Yes, unless not required by trust.

Pour-over statute: The trust must be identified in the will. The terms of the trust must be in a document other than the will and signed before or at the same time as the will.

Age of majority to be grantor or trustee: 18.

Rule against perpetuities: The common-law rule applies, but court may change a trust to make it valid.

Forms of property ownership: Common-law state. Tenancy in common, joint tenancy and tenancy by entirety recognized. Ownership by two or more persons presumes tenancy in common unless joint tenancy stated.

Joint bank accounts: Deposits payable to any survivor.

Montana

Uniform acts adopted: Uniform Probate Code; Uniform Trustees' Powers Act; Uniform Testamentary Additions to Trusts Act; Uniform Statutory Rule Against Perpetuities.

Must trustee be a state resident? No, but if out-of-state trustee is appointed, must qualify to do business in Montana.

Can creditors reach beneficiary's income? Yes. If spendthrift trust, income and principal are reachable when due and payable. If trust is limited to income and principal is necessary for education or support of the beneficiary, then creditor cannot compel trustee to pay anything.

Must the trust be in writing? Yes.

Must trustee post bond? No provision.

Pour-over statute: The trust must be identified in the will. The terms of the trust must be in a document other than the will and signed before or at the same time as the will.

Age of majority to be grantor or trustee: 18.

Rule against perpetuities: The common-law rule is modified by wait-and-see approach.

Forms of property ownership: Common-law state. Partnership interests, tenancy in common and joint tenancy (called "interests in common" and "joint interests") recognized. No tenancy by entirety in personal property. Tenancy in common presumed unless joint tenancy stated.

Joint bank accounts: Deposits payable to any survivor.

Note: Trust is irrevocable unless power to revoke is stated.

Nebraska

Uniform acts adopted: Uniform Probate Code; Uniform Testamentary Additions to Trusts Act; Uniform Statutory Rule Against Perpetuities.

Must trustee be a state resident? No, but if out-of-state trustee is appointed, must qualify to do business in Nebraska.

Can creditors reach beneficiary's income? Yes. No information found on spendthrift trusts.

Must the trust be in writing? A trust holding real estate must be in writing.

Must trustee post bond? No, unless required by trust.

Pour-over statute: The trust must be identified in the will. The terms of the trust must be in a document other than the will and signed before or at the same time as the will.

Age of majority to be grantor or trustee: 18.

Rule against perpetuities: The common-law rule is modified by wait-and-see approach.

Forms of property ownership: Common-law state. Tenancy in common and joint tenancy recognized. No tenancy by entirety.

Joint bank accounts: Deposits payable to any survivor unless
   clear and convincing evidence exists that deposit is payable
   only to specified survivor(s).

Nevada

Uniform acts adopted: Uniform Testamentary Additions to
   Trusts Act; Uniform Statutory Rule Against Perpetuities.
Must trustee be a state resident? No provision.
Can creditors reach beneficiary's income? Yes. If spendthrift
   trust, income is not reachable by creditors.
Must the trust be in writing? A trust holding real estate must be
   in writing.
Must trustee post bond? No, unless required by trust or ordered
   by court.
Pour-over statute: The trust must be identified in the will. The
   terms of the trust must be in a document other than the will
   and signed before or at the same time as the will.
Age of majority to be grantor or trustee: 18.
Rule against perpetuities: The common-law rule is modified by
   wait-and-see approach.
Forms of property ownership: Community property state.
   Tenancy in common, joint tenancy and community property
   recognized. No tenancy by entirety.
Joint bank accounts: Deposits payable to any survivor.
Note: If grantor states in the trust that it is irrevocable, then it is
   irrevocable for all purposes even if grantor is also beneficiary.

New Hampshire

Uniform acts adopted: Uniform Trustees' Powers Act; Uniform
   Testamentary Additions to Trusts Act.
Must trustee be a state resident? No, but if out-of-state trustee is
   appointed, a resident agent must also be appointed.
Can creditors reach beneficiary's income? Yes. If spendthrift
   trust, income is reachable when due and payable.
Must the trust be in writing? A trust holding real estate must be
   in writing.
Must trustee post bond? No, unless required by trust or ordered
   by court.
Pour-over statute: The trust must be identified in the will. The
   terms of the trust must be in a document other than the will
   and signed before or at the same time as the will.
Age of majority to be grantor or trustee: 18.

Rule against perpetuities: Wait-and-see approach; common-law rule is modified by actual rather than possible events.

Forms of property ownership: Common-law state. Tenancy in common presumed unless joint tenancy stated. Ownership by spouses creates joint tenancy. No tenancy by entirety.

Joint bank accounts: Deposits payable to any survivor.

New Jersey

Uniform acts adopted: Uniform Probate Code; Uniform Testamentary Additions to Trusts Act; Uniform Statutory Rule Against Perpetuities.

Must trustee be a state resident? No.

Can creditors reach beneficiary's income? Yes. If spendthrift trust, income and principal can be reached when due and payable.

Must the trust be in writing? A trust holding real estate must be in writing.

Must trustee post bond? If not the appointed trustee, if the trust requires it or if court orders it.

Pour-over statute: The trust must be identified in the will. The terms of the trust must be in a document other than the will and signed before or at the same time as the will.

Age of majority to be grantor or trustee: 18.

Rule against perpetuities: The common-law rule is modified by wait-and-see approach.

Forms of property ownership: Common-law state. Tenancy in common, joint tenancy and tenancy by entirety recognized. Ownership by spouses presumes tenancy by entirety unless stated otherwise. Tenancy in common presumed unless joint tenancy stated.

Joint bank accounts: Deposits payable to any survivor.

Note: Trust can be modified if power to revoke is not included.

New Mexico

Uniform acts adopted: Uniform Probate Code; Uniform Trustees' Powers Act; Uniform Testamentary Additions to Trusts Act.

Must trustee be a state resident? No.

Can creditors reach beneficiary's income? Yes. If spendthrift trust, income cannot be reached by creditors.

Must the trust be in writing? A trust holding real estate must be in writing.

Must trustee post bond? No, unless required by trust.

Pour-over statute: The trust must be identified in the will. The

terms of the trust must be in a document other than the will and signed before or at the same time as the will.

Age of majority to be grantor or trustee: 18.

Rule against perpetuities: Wait-and-see approach; common-law rule is modified by actual rather than possible events.

Forms of property ownership: Community property state. Tenancy in common, joint tenancy and community property recognized. Spouses may hold real estate as joint tenants. No tenancy by entirety.

Joint bank accounts: Deposits payable to any survivor unless clear and convincing evidence exists that deposit is payable only to specified survivor(s).

New York

Uniform acts adopted: Uniform Testamentary Additions to Trusts Act.

Must trustee be a state resident? No.

Can creditors reach beneficiary's income? Yes. If spendthrift trust, surplus income not slated for education or support can be reached, income and principal can be reached if beneficiary is also grantor, or income can be reached to pay taxes and to pay for necessities provided to beneficiary by creditor.

Must the trust be in writing? Yes.

Must trustee post bond? No, unless required by trust.

Pour-over statute: The trust must be identified in the will. The terms of the trust must be in a document other than the will and signed before or at the same time as the will.

Age of majority to be grantor or trustee: 18.

Rule against perpetuities: The common-law rule applies, with certain modifications designed to eliminate invalidity in specified cases.

Forms of property ownership: Common-law state. Tenancy in common, joint tenancy and tenancy by entirety recognized. Joint ownership by spouses presumes tenancy by entirety unless specified otherwise. Joint ownership by couples not legally married but who are described as husband and wife presumes joint tenancy unless tenancy in common stated. Tenancy in common presumed unless joint tenancy stated. Tenancy by entirety in personal property not recognized.

Joint bank accounts: Deposits payable to any survivor.

North Carolina

Uniform acts adopted: Uniform Testamentary Additions to Trusts Act.

Must trustee be a state resident? No, but if out-of-state trustee is appointed, a resident agent must also be appointed.

Can creditors reach beneficiary's income? Yes. If spendthrift trust, income can be reached when due and payable or to satisfy alimony or child support payments.

Must the trust be in writing? A trust holding real estate must be in writing.

Must trustee post bond? If not the appointed trustee. Otherwise, not unless required by trust or ordered by court.

Pour-over statute: The trust must be identified in the will. The terms of the trust must be in a document other than the will and signed before or at the same time as the will.

Age of majority to be grantor or trustee: 18.

Rule against perpetuities: The common-law rule applies.

Forms of property ownership: Common-law state. Tenancy in common, joint tenancy and tenancy by entirety recognized. Tenancy by entirety in personal property not recognized.

Joint bank accounts: Deposits payable to any survivor.

North Dakota

Uniform acts adopted: Uniform Probate Code; Uniform Testamentary Additions to Trusts Act; Uniform Statutory Rule Against Perpetuities.

Must trustee be a state resident? No provision.

Can creditors reach beneficiary's income? Yes. If spendthrift trust, creditors cannot reach the amount necessary for education and support of beneficiary.

Must the trust be in writing? A trust holding real estate must be in writing.

Must trustee post bond? No provision.

Pour-over statute: The trust must be identified in the will. The terms of the trust must be in a document other than the will and signed before or at the same time as the will.

Age of majority to be grantor or trustee: 18.

Rule against perpetuities: The common-law rule is modified by wait-and-see approach.

Forms of property ownership: Common-law state. Tenancy in common and joint tenancy recognized. No tenancy by entirety.

Joint bank accounts: Deposits payable to any survivor.

Note: Trust is considered irrevocable unless authority to revoke is stated.

Ohio

Uniform acts adopted: Uniform Testamentary Additions to Trusts Act.

Must trustee be a state resident? No provision.

Can creditors reach beneficiary's income? Yes. If spendthrift trust, income can be reached to satisfy beneficiary's debts.

Must the trust be in writing? A trust holding real estate must be in writing.

Must trustee post bond? Yes, unless not required by trust.

Pour-over statute: The trust must be identified in the will. The terms of the trust must be in a document other than the will and signed before or at the same time as the will.

Age of majority to be grantor or trustee: 18.

Rule against perpetuities: The common-law rule is modified by wait-and-see approach.

Forms of property ownership: Common-law state. Tenancy in common, joint tenancy and tenancy by entirety recognized. If joint tenancy, must be stated.

Joint bank accounts: Deposits payable to any survivor.

Note: Trust is considered irrevocable unless authority to revoke is stated.

Oklahoma

Uniform acts adopted: Uniform Testamentary Additions to Trusts Act.

Must trustee be a state resident? No, but if out-of-state trustee is appointed, a resident agent must also be appointed.

Can creditors reach beneficiary's income? Yes. If spendthrift trust, income can be reached when due and payable, to satisfy alimony or child support payments or for necessities provided to beneficiary by creditor.

Must the trust be in writing? Yes.

Must trustee post bond? Yes, unless not required by trust.

Pour-over statute: The trust must be identified in the will. The terms of the trust must be in a document other than the will and signed before or at the same time as the will.

Age of majority to be grantor or trustee: 18.

Rule against perpetuities: The common-law rule applies, but court can modify trust to make it valid.

Forms of property ownership: Common-law state. Tenancy in common, joint tenancy and tenancy by entirety recognized. Rights of survivorship must be stated.

Joint bank accounts: Deposits payable to any survivor.

Oregon

Uniform acts adopted: Uniform Trustees' Powers Act; Uniform Testamentary Additions to Trusts Act; Uniform Statutory Rule Against Perpetuities.

Must trustee be a state resident? No provision.

Can creditors reach beneficiary's income? Yes. No information found on spendthrift trusts.

Must the trust be in writing? A trust holding real estate must be in writing.

Must trustee post bond? No provision.

Pour-over statute: The trust must be identified in the will. The terms of the trust must be in a document other than the will and signed before or at the same time as the will.

Age of majority to be grantor or trustee: 18.

Rule against perpetuities: The common-law rule is modified by wait-and-see approach.

Forms of property ownership: Common-law state. Tenancy in common and tenancy by entirety recognized. Right of survivorship must be stated.

Joint bank accounts: Deposits payable to any survivor unless clear and convincing evidence exists that deposit is payable only to specified survivor(s).

Pennsylvania

Uniform acts adopted: Uniform Probate Code; Uniform Testamentary Additions to Trusts Act.

Must trustee be a state resident? No.

Can creditors reach beneficiary's income? Yes. If spendthrift trust, income can be reached to satisfy alimony or child support payments.

Must the trust be in writing? Yes.

Must trustee post bond? No, unless required by trust or ordered by court.

Pour-over statute: The trust must be identified in the will. The terms of the trust must be in a document other than the will and signed before or at the same time as the will.

Age of majority to be grantor or trustee: 18.

Rule against perpetuities: Wait-and-see approach; common-law rule is modified by actual rather than possible events.

Forms of property ownership: Common-law state. Tenancy in common and tenancy by entirety recognized. Joint tenancy with right of survivorship only if stated. Real estate jointly owned by spouses presumes tenancy by entirety unless stated otherwise. Tenancy by entirety in personal property recognized.

Joint bank accounts: Deposits payable to any survivor.

Puerto Rico

Uniform acts adopted: None.

Must trustee be a state resident? No.

Can creditors reach beneficiary's income? Yes. No information found on spendthrift trusts.

Must the trust be in writing? A trust holding real estate must be in writing.

Must trustee post bond? No, unless ordered by court.

Pour-over statute: The trust must be identified in the will. The terms of the trust must be in a document other than the will and signed before or at the same time as the will.

Age of majority to be grantor or trustee: 21.

Rule against perpetuities: A trust is void if there is an established order of succession extending beyond the lives of two persons in being.

Forms of property ownership: Community property jurisdiction. Co-ownership, community and conjugal property recognized. Property acquired during marriage belongs to both spouses in equal parts; property is presumed to belong to the marriage. Each spouse may dispose of half of community property by will.

Joint bank accounts: No provision.

Note: Trust is considered irrevocable unless power to revoke is stated.

Rhode Island

Uniform acts adopted: None.

Must trustee be a state resident? No provision.

Can creditors reach beneficiary's income? Yes. No information found on spendthrift trusts.

Must the trust be in writing? A trust holding real estate must be in writing.

Must trustee post bond? No provision.

Pour-over statute: The trust must be identified in the will. The terms of the trust must be in a document other than the will and signed before or at the same time as the will.

Age of majority to be grantor or trustee: 18.

Rule against perpetuities: Wait-and-see approach; common-law rule is modified by actual rather than possible events.

Forms of property ownership: Common-law state. Tenancy in common presumed unless stated otherwise. Tenancy in common, joint tenancy and tenancy by entirety recognized.

Joint bank accounts: Deposits payable to any survivor.

South Carolina

Uniform acts adopted: Uniform Probate Code; Uniform Trustees' Powers Act; Uniform Testamentary Additions to Trusts Act; Uniform Statutory Rule Against Perpetuities.

Must trustee be a state resident? No, but if out-of-state corporate trustee is appointed, must have capital of at least $250,000. All out-of-state trustees must qualify to do business in South Carolina.

Can creditors reach beneficiary's income? Yes. If spendthrift trust, court has jurisdiction to hear matters concerning attachments of trust by creditors.

Must the trust be in writing? Yes.

Must trustee post bond? No, unless required by trust.

Pour-over statute: The trust must be identified in the will. The terms of the trust must be in a document other than the will and signed before or at the same time as the will.

Age of majority to be grantor or trustee: 18.

Rule against perpetuities: The common-law rule is modified by wait-and-see approach.

Forms of property ownership: Common-law state. Tenancy in common and joint tenancy recognized. Right of survivorship only if stated. No tenancy by entirety.

Joint bank accounts: Deposits payable to any survivor.

South Dakota

Uniform acts adopted: Uniform Testamentary Additions to Trusts Act.

Must trustee be a state resident? No provision.

Can creditors reach beneficiary's income? Yes. If spendthrift trust, income can be reached only when due and payable.

Must the trust be in writing? A trust holding real estate must be in writing. A trust holding personal or other property may be written or oral.

Must trustee post bond? No provision.

Pour-over statute: The trust must be identified in the will. The terms of the trust must be in a document other than the will and signed before or at the same time as the will.

Age of majority to be grantor or trustee: 18.

Rule against perpetuities: Wait-and-see approach followed.

Forms of property ownership: Common-law state. Tenancy in common and joint tenancy recognized. No tenancy by entirety. Creditors' rights preserved against surviving joint owner(s).

Joint bank accounts: Deposits payable to any survivor.

Note: Trust is irrevocable unless authority to revoke is stated.

Tennessee

Uniform acts adopted: Uniform Testamentary Additions to Trusts Act.

Must trustee be a state resident? No, but if out-of-state trustee is appointed, must qualify to do business in Tennessee.

Can creditors reach beneficiary's income? Yes. If spendthrift trust, income can be reached when due and payable.

Must the trust be in writing? A trust may be oral or written. If oral, trust must be proven by clear and convincing evidence.

Must trustee post bond? No, unless required by trust.

Pour-over statute: The trust must be identified in the will. The terms of the trust must be in a document other than the will and signed before or at the same time as the will.

Age of majority to be grantor or trustee: 18.

Rule against perpetuities: The common-law rule applies.

Forms of property ownership: Common-law state. Tenancy in common and tenancy by entirety recognized.

Joint bank accounts: Deposits payable to any survivor.

Texas

Uniform acts adopted: Uniform Testamentary Additions to Trusts Act.

Must trustee be a state resident? No provision.

Can creditors reach beneficiary's income? Yes. If spendthrift trust, income cannot be reached by creditors.

Must the trust be in writing? Yes.

Must trustee post bond? Yes, if corporate trustee. Otherwise, not unless required by trust.

Pour-over statute: The trust must be identified in the will. The terms of the trust must be in a document other than the will and signed before or at the same time as the will.

Age of majority to be grantor or trustee: 18.

Rule against perpetuities: The common-law rule applies.

Forms of property ownership: Community property state. All property acquired by either spouse during marriage is community property. Tenancy in common recognized. No tenancy by entirety.

Joint bank accounts: Deposits payable to any survivor.

Note: Trust can be modified unless made irrevocable.

Utah

Uniform acts adopted: Uniform Probate Code; Uniform Trustees' Powers Act; Uniform Testamentary Additions to Trusts Act.

Must trustee be a state resident? No, but if out-of-state trustee is appointed, must qualify to do business in Utah.

Can creditors reach beneficiary's income? Yes. No information found on spendthrift trusts.

Must the trust be in writing? A trust holding real estate must be in writing.

Must trustee post bond? No, unless required by trust, requested by beneficiaries or ordered by the court.

Pour-over statute: The trust must be identified in the will. The terms of the trust must be in a document other than the will and signed before or at the same time as the will.

Age of majority to be grantor or trustee: 18.

Rule against perpetuities: The common-law rule applies.

Forms of property ownership: Common-law state. Tenancy in common, joint tenancy and tenancy by entirety recognized. Real estate presumed to be in tenancy in common. Joint tenancy only if stated.

Joint bank accounts: Deposits payable to any survivor.

Vermont

Uniform acts adopted: Uniform Testamentary Additions to Trusts Act.

Must trustee be a state resident? No, but if out-of-state trustee is appointed, a resident agent must also be appointed.

Can creditors reach beneficiary's income? Yes. If spendthrift trust, income can be reached when due and payable.

Must the trust be in writing? A trust holding real estate must be in writing; otherwise may be written or oral.

Must trustee post bond? Yes, unless not required by trust.

Pour-over statute: The trust must be identified in the will. The terms of the trust must be in a document other than the will and signed before or at the same time as the will.

Age of majority to be grantor or trustee: 18.

Rule against perpetuities: Wait-and-see approach; common-law rule is modified by actual rather than possible events.

Forms of property ownership: Common-law state. Tenancy is common, tenancy by entirety and joint tenancy recognized. The presumption is real estate is held by tenancy in common rather than joint tenancy unless otherwise stated.

Joint bank accounts: Deposits payable to any survivor.

Virgin Islands

Uniform acts adopted: None.

Must trustee be a state resident? No.

Can creditors reach beneficiary's income? Yes. No information found on spendthrift trusts.

Must the trust be in writing? A trust holding real estate must be in writing.

Must trustee post bond? No, unless required by trust.

Pour-over statute: No provision.

Age of majority to be grantor or trustee: 18.

Rule against perpetuities: No information found on rule against perpetuities.

Forms of property ownership: Common-law state. Tenancy in common, joint tenancy and tenancy by entirety recognized. Joint ownership by spouses presumes tenancy by entirety unless stated otherwise. Joint tenancy only if stated.

Joint bank accounts: No provision.

Virginia

Uniform acts adopted: None.

Must trustee be a state resident? No, but if out-of-state trustee is appointed, a resident agent must also be appointed unless trustee is a corporation authorized to do business in Virginia, or is a parent, sister or brother of decedent and has qualified to do business in Virginia.

Can creditors reach beneficiary's income? Yes. If spendthrift trust is under $500,000 in value and trustee has discretion to pay principal or income, trust cannot be reached by creditors as long as it was not created to defraud creditors.

Must the trust be in writing? A trust may be written or oral. Oral trusts holding real estate must be proven by clear and convincing evidence.

Must trustee post bond? No provision.

Pour-over statute: The trust must be identified in the will. The terms of the trust must be in a document other than the will and signed before or at the same time as the will.

Age of majority to be grantor or trustee: 18.

Rule against perpetuities: The common-law rule is modified by wait-and-see apprach

Forms of property ownership: Common-law state. Joint tenancy only where right of survivorship is stated. Tenancy in common and tenancy by entirety recognized.

Joint bank accounts: Deposits payable to any survivor unless clear and convincing evidence exists that deposit is payable only to specified survivor(s).

Washington

Uniform acts adopted: Uniform Testamentary Additions to Trusts Act.

Must trustee be a state resident? No provision.

Can creditors reach beneficiary's income? Yes. If spendthrift trust, income can be reached if court allows it or for necessities provided to beneficiary by creditor.

Must the trust be in writing? A trust holding real estate must be in writing. A trust holding personal property can be either oral or in writing.

Must trustee post bond? No provision.

Pour-over statute: The trust must be identified in the will. The terms of the trust must be in a document other than the will and signed before or at the same time as the will.

Age of majority to be grantor or trustee: 18.

Rule against perpetuities: Wait-and-see approach; common-law rule is modified by actual rather than possible events.

Forms of property ownership: Community property state. Tenancy in common and joint tenancy recognized. Joint tenancy with right of survivorship created if stated. No survivorship rights in tenancy by entirety. Property acquired during marriage is community property. Surviving spouse is entitled to all community property if deceased did not otherwise dispose of it by will.

Joint bank accounts: Deposits payable to any survivor unless evidence exists that deposit is payable only to specified survivor(s). This is subject to community property rights upon death of depositor.

West Virginia

Uniform acts adopted: Uniform Testamentary Additions to Trusts Act.

Must trustee be a state resident? No.

Can creditors reach beneficiary's income? Yes. If spendthrift trust, income can be reached when due and payable or if beneficiary is also grantor.

Must the trust be in writing? Yes.

Must trustee post bond? No provision.

Pour-over statute: The trust must be identified in the will. The terms of the trust must be in a document other than the will and signed before or at the same time as the will.

Age of majority to be grantor or trustee: 18.

Rule against perpetuities: The common-law rule applies.

Forms of property ownership: Common-law state. Tenancy in common, joint tenancy and tenancy by entirety recognized. Right of survivorship created if stated.

Joint bank accounts: Deposits payable to any survivor.

Wisconsin

Uniform acts adopted: None.

Must trustee be a state resident? No, but if out-of-state trustee is appointed, must qualify to do business in Wisconsin.

Can creditors reach beneficiary's income? Yes. If spendthrift trust, the income can be reached when due and payable.

Must the trust be in writing? Yes.

Must trustee post bond? Yes, unless not required by trust or ordered by court.

Pour-over statute: The trust must be identified in the will. The terms of the trust must be in a document other than the will and signed before or at the same time as the will.

Age of majority to be grantor or trustee: 18.

Rule against perpetuities: The common-law rule cannot invalidate a trust if the trustee can buy and sell trust property.

Forms of property ownership: Community property state. Tenancy in common and joint tenancy recognized. Ownership by spouses presumes joint tenancy unless document states otherwise. No tenancy by entirety.

Joint bank accounts: Deposits payable to any survivor.

Wyoming

Uniform acts adopted: Uniform Trustees' Powers Act; Uniform Testamentary Additions to Trusts Act.

Must trustee be a state resident? No.

Can creditors reach beneficiary's income? No provision.

Must the trust be in writing? A trust holding real estate must be in writing.

Must trustee post bond? No provision.

Pour-over statute: The trust must be identified in the will. The terms of the trust must be in a document other than the will and signed before or at the same time as the will.

Age of majority to be grantor or trustee: 18.

Rule against perpetuities: The common-law rule applies.

Forms of property ownership: Common-law state. Tenancy in common, joint tenancy and tenancy by entirety recognized. Right of survivorship created if stated.

Joint bank accounts: Deposits payable to any survivor.

UNIFIED FEDERAL ESTATE AND GIFT TAX RATES

The following table gives the unified federal estate and gift tax rates for estates of people who have died after 1987. As discussed in Chapter 5, these taxes don't apply unless your taxable estate is worth $600,000 or more. In order to calculate the tax owed, you must first determine your taxable estate—your net worth minus liabilities and exempt amounts (funeral expenses, charitable gifts, any amount left to a surviving spouse). Then, check on the chart below for the tax owed on the taxable estate. Finally, subtract the tax credit for the amount that would be owed on the first $600,000 (about $192,000). Remember, this credit may be lower if you have given gifts of more than $10,000 per year per person during your life.

1 *If taxable estate is more than*	2 *But not more than*	3 *Tax owed on amounts in 1*	4 *Rate of tax on excess over amounts in 1*
$ 0	$ 10,000	$ 0	18%
10,000	20,000	1,800	20
20,000	40,000	3,800	22
40,000	60,000	8,200	24
60,000	80,000	13,000	26
80,000	100,000	18,200	28
100,000	150,000	23,800	30
150,000	250,000	38,800	32
250,000	500,000	70,800	34
500,000	750,000	155,800	37
750,000	1,000,000	248,300	39
1,000,000	1,250,000	345,800	41
1,250,000	1,500,000	448,300	43
1,500,000	2,000,000	555,800	45
2,000,000	2,500,000	780,800	49
2,500,000	—	1,025,800	50

STATE TAXES

Every state except Nevada imposes one or more of three types of tax on the transfer of the property of a deceased person. The three types—inheritance tax, estate tax and the credit estate tax—are discussed in detail in Chapter 5.

The *inheritance tax* rates listed below indicate the minimum and maximum percentages that are assessed in each state. The rate that applies to each specific case within a state depends on several factors, including the relationship of the beneficiary to the deceased person and the share distributed to a particular person.

For example, in Delaware, a spouse of a deceased person would not be taxed on the first $70,000 inherited—this amount is exempt. But, a spouse would have to pay 2 percent on any inheritance valued at more than $70,000. The percentage would increase up to 6 percent as the value of the inheritance increased. Exemptions are calculated after all claims, funeral costs, estate administration expenses and other allowable deductions are subtracted.

Some states that don't impose an inheritance tax do impose an *estate tax*. Estate taxes are based on the value of the estate and are calculated like federal estate taxes.

The *credit estate tax* applies only to the few estates with over $600,000 that owe federal estate taxes. It works like a rebate and does not increase your taxes. The tax is equal to the maximum federal credit the federal government allows for payment of state inheritance and estate taxes. The specific tax rate in your state depends on the value of the estate after subtracting all deductions, exemptions and other credits.

Because tax rates and exemption levels may change at any time, it is advisable to check the accuracy of the information for your state with your state department of revenue and taxation.

Alabama
Inheritance tax: None.
Estate tax: None.
Credit estate tax: Yes.
Special provisions: None.

Alaska
Inheritance tax: None.
Estate tax: None.
Credit estate tax: Yes.
Special provisions: None.

Arizona
Inheritance tax: None.
Estate tax: None.
Credit estate tax: Yes.
Special provisions: None.

Arkansas
Inheritance tax: None.
Estate tax: None.
Credit estate tax: Yes.
Special provisions: None.

California
Inheritance tax: None. Repealed for estates of persons dying after June 9, 1982.
Estate tax: None.
Credit estate tax: Yes.
Special provisions: None.

Colorado
Inheritance tax: None.
Estate tax: None.
Credit estate tax: Yes.
Special provisions: None.

Connecticut
Inheritance tax: Inheriting spouse, child or parent pays 3–8%; brother or sister pays 4–10%; all others pay 8–14%.
Property exempt from taxation: $300,000 for spouse; $50,000 for child or parent; $6,000 for brother or sister; $1,000 for all others.
Estate tax: None.
Credit estate tax: Yes.
Special provisions: No tax on estates inherited by spouses of persons dying after June 30, 1988. A 30% surtax is added to all inheritance taxes, plus 10% for estates of persons who died on or after July 1, 1983; this additional 10% is not assessed against farmland that is transferred to natural or adopted descendants of the deceased person.

Delaware
Inheritance tax: Inheriting spouse, child or parent pays

2–6%; other relatives pay 5–10%; all others pay 10–16%.

Property exempt from taxation: $70,000 for spouse; $25,000 for child or parent; $5,000 for other relatives; $1,000 for all others.

Estate tax: None.
Credit estate tax: Yes.
Special provisions: None.

District of Columbia

Inheritance tax: None. Repealed for estates of persons dying after April 1, 1987.
Estate tax: None.
Credit estate tax: Yes.
Special provisions: None.

Florida

Inheritance tax: None.
Estate tax: None.
Credit estate tax: Yes.
Special provisions: None.

Georgia

Inheritance tax: None.
Estate tax: None.
Credit estate tax: Yes.
Special provisions: None.

Hawaii

Inheritance tax: None. Repealed for estates of persons dying after June 30, 1983.
Estate tax: None.
Credit estate tax: Yes.
Special provisions: None.

Idaho

Inheritance tax: None. Repealed for estates of persons dying after January 1, 1989.
Estate tax: None.
Credit estate tax: Yes.
Special provisions: None.

Illinois

Inheritance tax: None. Repealed for estates of persons dying after December 31, 1982.
Estate tax: None.
Credit estate tax: Yes.
Special provisions: None.

Indiana

Inheritance tax: Inheriting spouse, child or parent pays 1–10%; brother or sister pays 7–15%; all others pay 10–20%.
Property exempt from taxation: All for spouse; $10,000 for minor child; $5,000 for parent and other children; $500 for all others.
Estate tax: None.
Credit estate tax: Yes.
Special provisions: None.

Iowa

Inheritance tax: Inheriting spouse, child or parent pays 1–8%; brother or sister pays 5–10%; all others pay 10–15%.
Property exempt from taxation: $120,000 for spouse; $50,000 for child; $15,000 for parent or grandchild; none for all others.
Estate tax: None.
Credit estate tax: Yes.
Special provisions: The spouse receives a credit of one third of the tax due on the estate of any person dying after January 1, 1986, increasing to two-thirds for the estates of persons dying after January 1, 1987. No tax on estates inherited by spouses of persons dying after January 1, 1988.

Kansas

Inheritance tax: Inheriting spouse, child or parent pays 1–5%; brother or sister pays 3–12.5%; all others pay 10–15%.

Property exempt from taxation: All for spouse; $30,000 for child or parent; $5,000 for brother or sister; none for all others.

Estate tax: None.

Credit estate tax: Yes.

Special provisions: None.

Kentucky

Inheritance tax: Inheriting spouse, child or parent pays 2–10%; brother or sister pays 4–16%; all others pay 6–16%.

Property exempt from taxation: $50,000 for spouse; $20,000 for child; $5,000 for parent; $1,000 for brother or sister; $500 for all others.

Estate tax: None.

Credit estate tax: Yes.

Special provisions: No tax on estates inherited by spouses of persons dying after August 1, 1985.

Louisiana

Inheritance tax: Inheriting spouse, child or parent pays 2–3%; brother or sister pays 5–7%; all others pay 5–10%.

Property exempt from taxation: $10,000 for spouse, child or parent (before 1985); $15,000 (1985); $20,000 (1986); $25,000 (1987 and thereafter); total exemption for spouse (1992 and thereafter); $1,000 for brother or sister; $500 for all others.

Estate tax: None.

Credit estate tax: Yes.

Special provisions: None.

Maine

Inheritance tax: None. Repealed for estates of persons dying after June 30, 1986. Until then, inheriting spouse, child or parent pays 5–10%; brother or sister pays 8–14%; all others pay 14–18%.

Property exempt from taxation: $50,000 for spouse; $25,000 for child or parent; $1,000 for all others.

Estate tax: None.

Credit estate tax: Yes.

Special provisions: None.

Maryland

Inheritance tax: Inheriting spouse, child or parent pays 1%; all others pay 10%.

Property exempt from taxation: Real property and first $100,000 of other property for spouse; $150 for all other persons.

Estate tax: None.

Credit estate tax: Yes.

Special provisions: None.

Massachusetts

Inheritance tax: None.

Estate tax: 5–16%.

Property exempt from taxation: Total exemption for all estates with net value of less than $200,000; all others, not more than $150,000 exemption.

Credit estate tax: Yes.

Special provisions: None.

Michigan

Inheritance tax: Inheriting spouse, child, parent, brother or sister pays 2–10%; all others pay 12–17%.

Property exempt from taxation: $65,000 for spouse plus $5,000 for each minor child who does not inherit property; $10,000 for child, parent, brother or sister; none for all others, except that Michigan charitable, religious and educational associations are entirely exempt.

Estate tax: None.

Credit estate tax: Yes.

Special provisions: In certain cases the entire amount transferred to a surviving spouse may be exempted.

Minnesota

Inheritance tax: None.

Estate tax: None.

Credit estate tax: Yes.

Special provisions: None.

Mississippi

Inheritance tax: None.

Estate tax: 1–16% (1982–September 30, 1988); 1.7–18.4% (October 1, 1988–September 30, 1989); 1.4–18.5% (October 1, 1989–September 30, 1990); 1–16% (on or after October 1, 1990).

Property exempt from taxation: $175,625 (1982–September 30, 1988); $400,000 (October 1, 1988–September 30, 1989); $500,000 (October 1, 1989–September 30, 1990);

$600,000 (on or after October 1, 1990).

Credit estate tax: Yes.

Special provisions: None.

Missouri

Inheritance tax: None.

Estate tax: None.

Credit estate tax: Yes.

Special provisions: None.

Montana

Inheritance tax: Inheriting spouse, child or parent pays 2–8%; brother or sister pays 4–16%; all others pay 8–32%.

Property exempt from taxation: All for spouse or child; $7,000 for parent; $1,000 for brother or sister; none for all others.

Estate tax: None.

Credit estate tax: Yes.

Special provisions: None.

Nebraska

Inheritance tax: Inheriting spouse, child, parent, brother or sister pays 1%; all others pay 6–18%.

Property exempt from taxation: $10,000 for spouse, child, parent, brother or sister; $500 for all others.

Estate tax: None.

Credit estate tax: Yes.

Special provisions: None.

Nevada

Inheritance tax: None.

Estate tax: None.

Credit estate tax: Yes.

Special provisions: None.

New Hampshire

Inheritance tax: Inheriting spouse, child or parent pays no tax; all others pay 15%.

Property exempt from taxation:
All for spouse, child or
parent; none for all others.
Estate tax: None.
Credit estate tax: Yes.
Special provisions: Homestead
exempt if used as a home.

New Jersey

Inheritance tax: Inheriting
spouse, child or parent pays
2–16%; brother or sister pays
11–16%; all others pay 15–16%.
Property exempt from taxation:
$15,000 for spouse, child or
parent; $500 for all others if
the inherited share is valued
at $500 or less.
Estate tax: None.
Credit estate tax: Yes.
Special provisions: No tax on
estates inherited by spouses
of persons dying after
December 31, 1984; or by
child or parent of persons
dying after June 30, 1988.

New Mexico

Inheritance tax: None.
Estate tax: None.
Credit estate tax: Yes.
Special provisions: None.

New York

Inheritance tax: None.
Estate tax: 2–21%.
Property exempt from taxation:
All for estates with net value
less than $200,000. To
determine the exemptions
that apply in any specific
case, contact the New York
Department of Taxation and
Revenue.
Credit estate tax: Yes.
Special provisions: None.

North Carolina

Inheritance tax: Inheriting
spouse, child or parent pays
1–12%; brother or sister pays
4–16%; all others pay 8–17%.
Property exempt from taxation:
All for spouse; $2,350 for
parent, minor child or
mentally or physically
incapacitated child (after
July 31, 1985); $8,150 (after
June 30, 1986); $14,150 (after
December 31, 1986); $20,150
(after December 31, 1987);
$26,150 (after December 31,
1988); none for all others.
Estate tax: None.
Credit estate tax: Yes.
Special provisions: If there is no
surviving spouse or if the
surviving spouse has not used
all of the allowed credit, the
remaining amount can be
transferred to certain others.
When two or more persons
are entitled to credit, it is
allocated on a pro rata basis.

North Dakota

Inheritance tax: None.
Estate tax: None.
Credit estate tax: Yes.
Special provisions: None.

Ohio

Inheritance tax: None.
Estate tax: 2–7%.
Property exempt from taxation:
$500,000 for surviving spouse;
$14,000 for each minor child;
$6,000 for each adult child;
$10,000 for all others.
Credit estate tax: Yes.
Special provisions: None.

Oklahoma

Inheritance tax: None.
Estate tax: 0.5–15%.
Property exempt from taxation:
  All for surviving spouse;
  $175,000 for parent, child or
  lineal descendants.
Credit estate tax: Yes.
Special provisions: None.

Oregon

Inheritance tax: 12%.
Estate tax: None.
Property exempt from taxation:
  $200,000 (1983–1984); $500,000
  (1985–1986); no tax after
  1986.
Credit estate tax: Yes.
Special provisions: Although the
  tax is called an inheritance
  tax, it has the effect of an
  estate tax because it is levied
  against the estate, not the
  heir.

Pennsylvania

Inheritance tax: Inheriting
  spouse, child or parent pays
  6%; all others pay 15%.
Property exempt from taxation:
  None.
Estate tax: None.
Credit estate tax: Yes.
Special provisions: None.

Puerto Rico

Inheritance tax: None.
Estate tax: None.
Credit estate tax: Yes.
Special provisions: None.

Rhode Island

Inheritance tax: None.
Estate tax: 2–9%.

Property exempt from taxation:
  $175,000 for a surviving
  spouse; otherwise, $25,000.
Credit estate tax: Yes.
Special provisions: None.

South Carolina

Inheritance tax: None.
Estate tax: 6–8%. Repealed for
  estates of persons dying after
  June 30, 1991.
Property exempt from taxation:
  Unlimited marital deduction
  for surviving spouse, similar
  to federal taxation rules;
  otherwise, $120,000 (on or
  before June 30, 1988);
  $140,000 (July 1, 1988–
  June 30, 1989); $175,000
  (July 1, 1989–June 30, 1990);
  $320,000 (July 1, 1990–
  June 30, 1991).
Credit estate tax: Yes.
Special provisions: None.

South Dakota

Inheritance tax: Inheriting
  spouse or child pays 1.5–7.5%;
  parent pays 3–15%; brother or
  sister pays 4–20%; all others
  pay 5–30%.
Property exempt from taxation:
  All for spouse; $30,000 for
  child; $3,000 for parent; $500
  for brother or sister; $200 for
  aunt, uncle or their
  descendants; $100 for all
  others.
Estate tax: None.
Credit estate tax: Yes.
Special provisions: None.

Tennessee

Inheritance tax: Inheriting
  spouse, child, parent, brother

or sister pays 5.5–9.5%; all others pay 6.5–16% (before 1986); 6–15% (1986); 5.5–13% (1987–1988; 5.5–9.5% (after 1988).

Property exempt from taxation: $325,000 for spouse, child, parent, brother or sister (1984); $400,000 (1985); $500,000 (1986); $600,000 (after 1986); $10,000 for all others (on or before June 30, 1984); $25,000 (July 1, 1984–December 31, 1984); $50,000 (1985); $100,000 (1986); $150,000 (1987); $250,000 (1988); $350,000 (1989); $600,000 (after 1989).

Estate tax: None.

Credit estate tax: Yes.

Special provisions: For spouse, child, parent, brother or sister, plus for certain others related by marriage, the exemptions increase each year following the schedule of federal tax exemption increases.

Texas

Inheritance tax: Inheriting spouse, child or parent pays 1–6%; brother or sister pays 3–10%; all others pay 5–20%.

Property exempt from taxation: Spouse, child and parent share one exemption up to $200,000 but not less than $25,000; $10,000 for brother or sister; $500 for all others.

Estate tax: None.

Credit estate tax: Yes.

Special provisions: None.

Utah

Inheritance tax: None.

Estate tax: None. Repealed for estates of persons dying after January 1, 1977.

Credit estate tax: Yes.

Special provisions: None.

Vermont

Inheritance tax: None.

Estate tax: None.

Credit estate tax: Yes.

Special provisions: None.

Virginia

Inheritance tax: None.

Estate tax: None.

Credit estate tax: Yes.

Special provisions: None.

Virgin Islands

Inheritance tax: Inheriting spouse, child or parent pays 2.5%; brother or sister pays 5%; all others pay 7.5%.

Property exempt from taxation: $50,000 for spouse, child or parent; $30,000 for brother or sister; $5,000 for all others.

Estate tax: None.

Credit estate tax: Yes.

Special provisions: None.

Washington

Inheritance tax: None. Repealed for estates of persons dying after December 31, 1982.

Estate tax: None.

Credit estate tax: Yes.

Special provisions: None.

West Virginia

Inheritance tax: None.

Property exempt from taxation: $30,000 for spouse; $10,000 for child, parent, brother or sister; $200 for all others.

Estate tax: None.
Credit estate tax: Yes.
Special provisions: None.

Wisconsin

Inheritance tax: Inheriting spouse, child or parent pays 2.5–12.5%; brother or sister pays 5–20%; all others pay 7.5–20%.
Property exempt from taxation: All for spouse; $10,000 for child or parent (before April 13, 1984); $25,000 April 13, 1984–June 30, 1985); $50,000 (after July 1, 1985); $1,000 for brother or sister; $500–$1,000 for all others.
Estate tax: None.
Credit estate tax: Yes.
Special provisions: None.

Wyoming

Inheritance tax: None. Repealed for estates of persons dying after December 31, 1982.
Estate tax: None.
Credit estate tax: Yes.
Special provisions: None.

WORKSHEET

I. FAMILY INFORMATION

Date of preparation _____

Husband   Wife

Name
_____   _____

Address
_____   _____

Phone number
_____   _____

Birth date
_____   _____

Social Security number
_____   _____

Employer
_____   _____

Address/Phone number
_____   _____

Child(ren)	Birth date	Social Security number
1. _____	_____	_____
2. _____	_____	_____
3. _____	_____	_____

Grandchild(ren)/ Other dependents	Birth date	Social Security number
1. _____	_____	_____
2. _____	_____	_____
3. _____	_____	_____

II. IMPORTANT FAMILY CONTACTS (include name, address and phone number)

Lawyer _____

Accountant _____

Bank officer _____

Clergy _____

Doctor _____

Insurance agent _____

Stockbroker _____

Executor _____

Trustee _____

Minor's guardian _____

III. FINANCIAL INFORMATION

A. *YOUR ASSETS*

Real estate (land, home, business property, condos, co-ops, etc.)

Description or address	Type of ownership (sole, joint, etc.)	Market value/Equity
_____	_____	_____
_____	_____	_____
_____	_____	_____

Cash or equivalent funds (checking accounts, savings accounts, money market accounts, certificates of deposit, etc.)

Type	Bank	Account number	Balance
_____	_____	_____	_____
_____	_____	_____	_____
_____	_____	_____	_____

Investments (stocks, bonds, mutual fund shares, other securities, etc.)

Type	Company	Number of shares	Market value
_____	_____	_____	_____
_____	_____	_____	_____
_____	_____	_____	_____

Personal property (you need not list individual items unless of significant value)

Description

_____

_____

Retirement plans (IRAs, pension plans, Keoghs, etc.)

Type	Name of plan	Beneficiary	Current value
_____	_____	_____	_____
_____	_____	_____	_____
_____	_____	_____	_____

Life insurance (also note the policy number and type of insurance coverage, such as whole or term)

Insured	Company	Beneficiary	Death benefit
_____	_____	_____	_____
_____	_____	_____	_____
_____	_____	_____	_____

Debts owed you (include name, address and phone number)

Who owes	Amount owed
_____	_____
_____	_____
_____	_____

B. *YOUR LIABILITIES*

Type	Company/Person owed	Amount owed	When due	Secured by
Mortgages	_____	_____	_____	_____
Installment loans	_____	_____	_____	_____
Education loans	_____	_____	_____	_____
Personal loans	_____	_____	_____	_____
Other debts	_____	_____	_____	_____

C. *FIGURING OUT YOUR NET WORTH*

	Amounts		
	Husband	Wife	Joint
ASSETS			
Real estate	_____	_____	_____
Cash or equivalent funds	_____	_____	_____
Investments	_____	_____	_____
Personal property	_____	_____	_____
Retirement plans	_____	_____	_____
Life insurance	_____	_____	_____
Debts owed you	_____	_____	_____
Total assets	_____	_____	_____

LIABILITIES

Mortgages   _____ _____ _____

Installment loans   _____ _____ _____

Education loans   _____ _____ _____

Personal loans   _____ _____ _____

Other debts   _____ _____ _____

Total liabilities _____ _____ _____

NET ESTATE   _____ _____ _____
  (assets minus liabilities)

IV. TRUST DECISIONS

Trustee(s)   _____

                                  _____

Successor trustee   _____

Alternate successor trustee   _____

Child beneficiary   _____

                                  _____

                                  _____

Other relative beneficiary   _____

                                  _____

Nonrelative beneficiary   _____

                                  _____

Charitable organization   _____
  beneficiary   _____

                                  _____

Alternate beneficiary   _____

TRUST SCHEDULE

This sample trust schedule shows how to list and describe assets placed into a living trust. If you are married, you can fill out separate forms for you and your spouse (Schedules A and B), or you can use one form to list your assets together, as in the example given on the following page.

Listing your assets (those with and without ownership papers) on a trust schedule serves two purposes: It helps you remember what you've placed in the trust; and it lets your trustee and beneficiaries know where your assets are—after you die.

To transfer personal possessions to a trust, you would use a general statement, such as "All of my personal property and household furnishings located at XYZ address."

To transfer assets with ownership papers, such as real estate, bank accounts, stocks and bonds, however, you *must* retitle them into the name of the trust. Simply listing titled assets on a trust schedule, without retitling them, is meaningless.

You should update your trust schedule after a major purchase or sale of assets or events such as a divorce or remarriage.

Schedule A

Husband	Wife	Joint	Market Value
		House and real estate located at 2121 Pleasant Way, Anytown, NY.	$325,000
		All personal property and household furnishings located at 2121 Pleasant Way, Anytown, NY.	$100,000
1989 Toyota Celica.	1990 Ford Taurus.		$3,500 and $11,000, respectively.
Summer house and real estate located at 901 Sun Valley Rd., Anytown, FL.			$125,000
		All personal property and household furnishings located at 901 Sun Valley Rd., Anytown, FL.	$45,000
	500 shares of AT&T stock, certificate No. 1234567. Certificates located in wife's personal file drawer.		$19,000
		Funds accrued in savings account No. 94350, held at First National City Bank of Anytown, Anytown, NY.	$56,000

Schedule A (*continued*)

Husband	Wife	Joint	Market Value
	IRA account No. 39340, held at XYZ Credit Union, Anytown, NY.		$7,500

LAST UPDATED: December 8, 1991

GLOSSARY

The following terms are used in this book. Italicized terms in definitions are themselves defined in other glossary entries.

Annuity trust   *Charitable remainder trust* that provides the *donor* a fixed annual income.

Assets   Money and *real* or *personal property* owned by a person or organization.

Bank account trust   Another name for a *Totten trust.*

Beneficial interest   Right to enjoy or profit from property held in *trust;* the person with the beneficial interest is the *beneficiary.*

Beneficiary   Person who is named to receive some benefit or money from a legal document such as a *trust,* life insurance policy or *will.*

Bequest   Gift of *personal property* left in a *will.*

Bond   Monetary guarantee that, should a *trustee* steal trust funds, compensation will be awarded up to the bond's limit.

Bypass trust   *Trust* typically created by a married couple to contain property that will not be included, for *estate tax* purposes, in the *estate* of the surviving spouse. The surviving spouse receives *income* from the trust but not the *principal.*

Charitable lead trust   *Trust* that donates to a charity *income* from trust *assets* while reserving the assets for later distribution to other *beneficiaries.* Compare with *charitable remainder trust.*

Charitable remainder trust   *Trust* that pays *income* from trust *assets* to the *donor* or *beneficiaries* while reserving the assets for later contribution to a charity. Compare with *charitable lead trust.*

Community property Property acquired during marriage that was not a *gift* to or inheritance of one spouse or specifically kept separate.

Contingent interest Interest in property that is dependent on the occurrence of a future event, such as a college graduation, not on the passage of time.

Corpus Latin for "body"; the main part of a thing (like a *trust* or *will*); for example, the *principal* placed in a trust.

Court trust Another term for a *testamentary trust.*

Creator Person who creates a *trust* by providing money or property for it; see also *donor, grantor, settlor, trustor.*

Credit estate tax State tax on the assets of someone who has died. Applies only in some states and only to estates that are required to pay federal estate taxes. Estate does not pay double taxes but instead, by paying a credit estate tax, rebates part of the federal estate tax owed back to the state.

Creditor Person or corporation to whom money is due.

Credit shelter trust Another name for *bypass trust.*

Death tax Another name for *inheritance* and *estate taxes.*

Decedent Person who has died.

Donee Recipient of a *gift, trust* or power left in a trust; *beneficiary* of a trust.

Donor Person or corporation that gives a *gift* to or confers a power on another; *creator* of a *trust.*

Durable power of attorney Legal document whereby one person authorizes another to make medical and financial decisions should illness or incapacitation occur.

Estate All property, *real* or *personal,* that a person owns.

Estate tax Type of *death tax* based on the *decedent*'s right to transfer property; not a tax on the property itself.

Executor Person or corporation appointed in a *will* or by a court to settle the *estate* of a deceased person (female gender, *executrix*).

Family pot trust *Trust* that pools *assets* for distribution to several children based on need.

Family trust Another name for a *bypass trust.*

Federal estate tax Federal tax assessed against the *assets* of a person who has died if the value of the taxable assets exceeds $600,000.

Fiduciary Person in a position of trust and confidence; a person who has a duty to act primarily for the benefit of another. A *trustee* or *executor* acts as a fiduciary.

Future interest   Interest in property that cannot be possessed or enjoyed until a specified period of time passes or a future event (for example, a 21st birthday) occurs.

Generation-skipping trust   *Trust* designed to skip one generation of estate taxes because the trust leaves the *principal* to the *grantor*'s grandchildren, not the grantor's children.

Gift   Voluntary lifetime or at-death transfer of property, made without compensation.

Gift tax   Tax on lifetime transfers of property given without consideration or for less consideration than the property is worth.

Grantor   Another term for *creator* of a trust. See also *donor, settlor, trustor.*

Grantor trust   *Living trust* in which the *grantor* maintains enough control over the *assets* so that the trust income received is taxed to the grantor, not to the trust or to the trust's *beneficiaries.*

Gross estate   Property owned by a *decedent* at death.

Guardian   Person or corporation appointed by a court to handle the affairs or property of another who is unable to do so because of incapacity.

Heir   Person or corporation designated to inherit property from someone who has died.

Income   All financial gains from investments, work or business.

Income beneficiary   *Beneficiary* of a *trust* who receives only the income generated by the trust assets.

Inheritance tax   Tax imposed on property received by *beneficiaries* from the *estate* of a *decedent.*

Insurance trust   *Trust* that owns and manages a life insurance policy and designates its *beneficiaries.*

Intestate   Not leaving a valid *will.*

Irrevocable trust   *Trust* that cannot be changed or canceled after it is created.

Joint tenancy with right of survivorship   Form of ownership in which property is equally shared by all owners and is automatically transferred to the surviving owners when one of them dies.

Kiddie tax   1986 federal income tax reform that taxes all annual *income* above $1,000 paid to children under age 14 at the parents' tax rate.

Life estate   Property right limited to the lifetime of its holder, often *income* from an *estate.* This right cannot be passed to an *heir.*

Living (or *inter vivos*) trust   *Trust* that is set up and put into effect while its *creator* is living.

Living will A separate document in which a person, while competent to do so, expresses a wish that his or her life not be prolonged by artificial life support systems if his or her medical condition becomes hopeless.

Nonmarital trust Another name for a *bypass trust.*

Pay-on-death account Another name for a *Totten trust.*

Per capita *Will* or *trust* distribution plan that requires that all living descendants of the *grantor,* regardless of generation, receive an equal share of the grantor's estate.

Personal property Property that is movable, not land or things attached to land.

Personal representative Person named in a *will* or appointed by a court to settle an *estate.* Also called PR. See also *executor.*

Per stirpes *Will* or *trust* distribution plan that requires that descendants of a deceased *beneficiary,* as a group, inherit equal shares of the amount the deceased beneficiary would have received had he or she lived. (For example, if your child predeceases you, any grandchildren descended from that child would receive equal shares of your deceased child's inheritance.)

Pooled-income fund *Charitable remainder trust* managed by a charity in which contributions from several *donors* are combined and managed jointly. Typically, donors or their designated *beneficiaries* receive income for life or a specified time from the pooled funds proportionate to their contribution.

Pour-over will *Will* provision that distributes money or property to a *trust* that already exists.

Power of appointment Power given in a *trust* to a person (known as the *donee*) to dispose of the *grantor*'s property. A power of appointment can be "general" or "limited." If general, the donee can give the property to anyone, including him or herself. If limited, the property must go to someone other than the donee or the donee's *estate.*

Present interest Right to use property immediately. Compare with *future interest.*

Principal Property in a *trust;* also called *corpus.*

Probate Legal process of establishing the validity of a deceased person's last *will* and testament; commonly refers to the process and laws for settling an *estate.*

QTIP (Qualified terminable interest property) trust *Trust* that qualifies for the *unlimited marital deduction* and postpones payment of any *estate taxes* owed until both spouses have died.

The surviving spouse receives *trust income* for life but has little or no legal right to the trust's *principal.*

Real property   Property that's immovable, such as land, buildings and whatever else is attached to or growing on land.

Removal clause   Provision in a *trust* describing how and for what reasons a *trustee* may be removed.

Res   Subject matter or contents of a *trust* or *will;* see also *corpus, principal.*

Resident agent   Person living in a state who is authorized to accept legal documents on behalf of another.

Residual beneficiary   Person who receives remaining property that has not been given away in a *trust* or *will,* or person who receives property only after the original *beneficiary* has died.

Residuary trust   Another name for *bypass trust.*

Revocable trust   *Trust* that can be taken back, canceled or changed.

Section 2503(c) trust   *Trust* that allows a *grantor* to make *gifts* of $10,000 a year to a trust for the future benefit of minor children without the grantor incurring *gift taxes.*

Settlor   Another term for *creator* of a trust. See also *grantor, donor.*

Spendthrift clause   Provision included in some trusts that prohibits the *beneficiary* from giving or selling to others the beneficiary's rights to the trust's *assets* or *income.*

Standby trust   *Living trust* that takes effect if a *grantor* becomes ill or incapacitated or dies. The grantor's *assets* are transferred to the trust and managed by the designated *trustee.*

Successor trustee   Person who takes over the rights and responsibilities of an original *trustee.*

Tenancy by entirety   Form of spousal ownership in which property is equally shared and automatically transferred to the surviving spouse. While both spouses are living, ownership of the property can be altered only by divorce or mutual agreement.

Tenancy in common   Way of jointly owning property in which each person's share passes to his or her *heirs* or *beneficiaries,* but the ownership shares need not be equal.

Testamentary trust   *Trust* established in a person's *will.*

Testate   Dying with a valid *will.*

Title   Ownership of property, or the document that shows ownership.

Totten trust   *Revocable trust* created by the owner of a bank account (checking, savings or other) for the future benefit of another.

Trust   Real or personal property held by one party (the *trustee*) for the benefit of another (the *beneficiary*).

Trust B   Another name for *bypass trust.*

Trustee   Person who holds and/or manages money or property for the benefit of another.

Trust instrument   Written statement creating any type of *trust.*

Trustor   Term used for the *creator* of a *testamentary trust.*

Unitrust   *Charitable remainder trust* that provides the *donor* a fluctuating annual income based on investment performance.

Unlimited marital deduction   Allows a spouse to transfer all property to his or her spouse without *federal estate tax.*

Vest   To grant immediate and full ownership rights.

Will   Legal document that declares how a person wishes property to be distributed to *heirs* or *beneficiaries* after death.

Will trust   Another term for a *testamentary trust.*

BIBLIOGRAPHY AND RESOURCES

BOOKS

Avoiding Probate: Tamper-Proof Estate Planning, by Cliff Roberson. Tab Books, Inc., 13311 Monterey Ave., Blue Ridge Summit, PA 17294-0850. 1989. 263 pages. $14.95.

Information on probate-avoidance techniques, including revocable living trusts, life insurance and joint tenancy. Also discusses wills, living wills and getting professional help.

Estate Planning Made Easy, by Herbert F. Starr. Tab Books, Inc., 13311 Monterey Ave., Blue Ridge Summit, PA 17294-0850. 1989 (2nd Ed.). 192 pages. $14.95.

Recently updated. Explains estate-planning concepts in nontechnical language. Limited information on trusts, but does include a sample trust schedule.

Estate Planning—A Practical Guide to Wills, Trusts, Probate and Death Taxes for Everyone, Homestead Publishing Co., 4455 Torrance Blvd., Suite 220, Torrance, CA 90503-4392. 1988. 320 pages. $42.95.

Information on how to plan your estate. Detailed information on trusts. Includes an estate-planning worksheet, sample wills and trusts.

How to Avoid Probate, Updated!, by Norman F. Dacey. Macmillan Publishing Co., Front and Brown Sts., Riverside, NJ 08075. 1990. 598 pages. $16.95.

Contains do-it-yourself living trust forms for avoiding probate in a multitude of situations. Forms updated regularly. Will forms also included.

How to Prepare Your Own Living Trust for a Small Estate, by John F. Goodson. The Forms Man, Inc., Law Forms, Inc., 10 Darius Ct., Dix Hills, NY 11746. 1990. 143 pages. $24.95.
Valid in all 50 states. For individuals and couples with property valued between $30,000 and $600,000. Includes a manual plus all the required forms to prepare a living trust.

How to Set Up Your Own Living Trust to Avoid Probate, DSA Financial Publishing Corp., 708 12th St. NW, Canton, OH 44703. 1988 (2nd Ed.). 81 pages. $19.95.
Information on establishing a living trust. Includes blank forms. Author advises readers to have forms reviewed by professional.

Introduction to Estate Planning, by Chris J. Prestopino. Kendall-Hunt, 2460 Kerper Blvd., Dubuque, IA 52001. 1992. 640 pages. $44.95.
A recently updated textbook. Author gives an overview of estate-planning concepts and tax information and illustrates specific strategies with examples and charts. Extensive glossary.

The Living Trust Handbook, by David E. Miller. David E. Miller Law Corp., 601 Van Ness Ave., Suite 2050, San Francisco, CA 94102. 1991. 210 pages. $20.00.
Discusses why wills, joint tenancy and gift giving are less desirable estate-planning tools than revocable living trusts. Forms not included.

The Living Trust: The Failproof Way to Pass Along Your Estate to Your Heirs Without Lawyers, Courts or the Probate System, by Henry W. Abts III. Contemporary Books Inc., 180 N. Michigan Ave., Chicago, IL 60601. 1989. 304 pages. $19.95.
This guide is devoted to the topic of revocable living trusts. Includes numerous examples to help illustrate the various situations in which a living trust is used. Sample trust forms not included.

Loving Trust: The Smart, Flexible Alternative to Wills and Probate, by Robert A. Esperti and Renno L. Peterson. Penguin Books, 375 Hudson St., New York, NY 10014. 1991. 318 pages. $12.95.
Recommends the use of revocable living trusts over wills and probate-avoidance tools such as joint tenancy. Forms not included.

Plan Your Estate: Wills, Probate Avoidance, Trusts and Taxes, by Denis Clifford. Nolo Press, 950 Parker St., Berkeley, CA 94710. 1989 (National Ed.). 380 pages. $17.95.
A plain-language discussion of estate planning. Topics include wills, the role of trusts in estate planning, making gifts, reducing your tax liability, planning for incapacitation and more. Includes sample will and revocable living trust forms.

Probate: Settling an Estate: A Step-by-Step Guide, by Kay Ostberg in association with HALT. Random House, 201 E. 50th St., New York, NY 10022. 1990. 162 pages. $8.95.
A "how-to" book for handling probate from start to finish. Includes a list of probate rules and death tax rates for each state and a check list of the tasks that need to be done.

A Report on Probate: Consumer Perspectives and Concerns, by Michael J. Klug. American Association of Retired Persons, 609 E St. NW, Washington, DC 20049. 1990. 39 pages. Free.
An academic paper that evaluates America's probate system. Looks at the cost of probate, the effectiveness of three different probate fee systems and whether recent reforms adequately address consumers' concerns.

Scott on Trusts, by Austin W. Scott and William F. Fratcher. Little, Brown & Co., Law Division, 34 Beacon St., Boston, MA 02108. 1991. 12 volumes. Available in libraries.
Written by lawyers as a reference guide for lawyers. Filled with detailed information on estate planning and trusts.

Trusts, by George T. Bogert. West Publishing Co., 50 W. Kellogg Blvd., St. Paul, MN 55164-0526. 1987 (National Ed.). 950 pages. Available in libraries.
Also intended for lawyers but written in plain language. Includes exhaustive list of cases.

Understanding Living Trusts, by Vickie Schumacher and Jim Schumacher. Schumacher & Co., 2049 Century Park E., Suite 410, Los Angeles, CA 90067. 1990. 209 pages. $19.95.
A guide to revocable and irrevocable living trusts. Includes information on selecting trustees and beneficiaries, transferring assets and updating a trust. Also discusses life insurance and charitable and marital trusts. No trust forms. Printed in large type.

The Way of Wills: Trust and Estate Planning for Government Employees, by G. Jerry Shaw, Thomas J. O'Rourke and Virginia Hurt Johnson. MPC Publications, 715 8th St. SE, Suite 300, Washington, DC 20003. 1990. 120 pages. $10.00.

Explains how to plan your estate and devotes four chapters to different kinds of trusts. Written specifically for federal workers. Includes glossary.

You Can't Take It with You: A Step-by-Step, Personalized Approach to Your Will to Avoid Probate and Estate Taxes, by David C. Larsen. Vintage Press–Random House, 201 E. 50th St., New York, NY 10022. 1988. 139 pages. $6.95.

Explains how to avoid probate and taxes through the use of trusts. Includes sample language for both living and testamentary trusts.

LEGAL SOFTWARE

Nolo's Living Trust, by Mary Randolph. Nolo Press, 950 Parker St., Berkeley, CA 94710. 1991 (1st National Ed.). $79.95.

A Macintosh- and IBM-compatible program. This software lets nonlawyers create a revocable living trust to avoid probate in every state but Louisiana. Comes with instruction manual.

TrustMaker, by Legisoft. 3430 Noriega, San Francisco, CA 94122. 1990. $99.00.

A Macintosh- and IBM-compatible program. This software lets nonlawyers create a legally valid revocable living trust in all 50 states. Comes with instruction manual.

WillMaker, by Legisoft. Nolo Press, 950 Parker St., Berkeley, CA 94710. 1990 (4th Ed.). $69.95.

A Macintosh- and IBM-compatible program. This software lets nonlawyers create a will in every state except Louisiana. Also helps you prepare testamentary trusts for people who can't handle their money (spendthrifts), disadvantaged people and groups of beneficiaries.

RESOURCES

You can write to the following organizations for more information on estate planning or for a referral to an estate-planning lawyer in your area:

HALT, Inc.
1319 F St. NW, Suite 300
Washington, DC 20004

Legal Counsel for the Elderly
601 E St. NW
Building A, 4th Floor
Washington, DC 20049

American College of Trust & Estate Counsel
3415 Sepulveda Blvd., Suite 460
Los Angeles, CA 90034
(310) 572-7280

Legal Counsel for the Elderly also offers legal hotlines in the following areas:

District of Columbia (202) 234-0970
Florida (800) 252-5997
Michigan (800) 347-LAWS
Ohio (800) 488-6070
Pennsylvania (800) 262-LAWS
Texas (800) 622-2520

Acknowledgments

HALT wishes to acknowledge the generous contributions it has received from the following individuals in support of this book:

H. Wayne Agnew
Robert F. Becker
George D. Braden
Richard I. Chiss
Sheila G. Cook
Luc and Françoise Delvaulx
Diane Lyons Fourton
Duane R. Kullberg
Richard Proskauer
Anita L. Stafford
John W. Vollmayer
Keith Wentz
John P. Williams
Gregory S. Windham

ABOUT THE AUTHORS

Theresa Meehan Rudy is Coordinator of Education Programs at HALT. She is the author of *Small Claims Court, Everyday Contracts, Fee Arbitration: Model Rules & Commentary* and "Arbitrating Lawyer-Client Fee Disputes: A National Survey." Ms. Rudy received her B.A. in 1981 from the University of Massachusetts, Amherst, and is a lay arbitrator for the District of Columbia Bar's fee and malpractice arbitration programs.

Kay Ostberg is the Deputy Director of HALT. She is the author of *Using a Lawyer, Probate, Everyday Contracts, If You Want to Sue a Lawyer* and the 1990 "Attorney Discipline National Survey and Report." Ms. Ostberg received her J.D. in 1983 from the National Law Center at George Washington University. She is a member of the National Federation of Paralegal Associations Advisory Board.

Jean Dimeo is a Washington, D.C.–based journalist. She is an award-winning business reporter and editor who covers pension, health care and insurance issues. Ms. Dimeo previously worked as a reporter for the Dallas *Times Herald.* She received her B.S. in journalism in 1984 from Bowling Green State University, Ohio.